The Legacy Journey

A Radical View of Biblical Wealth and Generosity

"A good man leaves an inheritance . . ."

PROVERBS 13:22

The Legacy Journey

A Radical View of Biblical Wealth and Generosity

DAVE RAMSEY

RAMSEY
PRESS

Editors: Allen Harris, Jennifer Gingerich
Cover Design: Melissa McKenney
Interior Design: Mandi Cofer

Printed in the United States of America
14 15 16 17 18 BVG 5 4 3 2 1

Dedication

To the wonderful Christians I have met around the world who take on the task of managing wealth for the good of God's kingdom. These wealthy men and women follow Christ and serve Him and His kingdom, but they seldom get accolades. On the contrary, they are often the target of hate, criticism, jealousy, and envy. They do most of their investing in God's kingdom without the media or the general public ever knowing their levels of giving. They are kind, compassionate, smart, and full of integrity. There are thousands of you, and I for one salute you and thank you for your example. I'm a more generous man—a better man—for knowing you.

Acknowledgments

This book is the result of years of thought, prayer, and study—and a lot of conversations. Special thanks to those who walked with me on this journey and helped make this book possible:

Sharon Ramsey, my ever-encouraging wife, girlfriend, and confidant.

Allen Harris, my editor, for helping me get this book out of my head and onto the page.

Preston Cannon, for coordinating and leading this project.

Jen Gingerich, for providing outstanding editorial and project management support.

Acknowledgments

Bob Bunn, for weeks' worth of faithful Bible scholarship and research.

Luke LeFevre, Brad Dennison, and Melissa McKenney, for overseeing all design elements and cover art.

Debbie LoCurto, Jen Sievertsen, Brent Spicer, Brian Williams, and Robbie Poe, for helping talk through early versions of this material.

Mike Glenn and Michael Easley, for their pastoral encouragement and careful review of early drafts of this book.

Contents

Contents

CHAPTER ONE

The Problem with God's Ways of Handling Money

The light was so blinding, I had to squint to see anything at all. It was a bright, sunny day, and the detailers had washed, waxed, and polished until the whole car was gleaming. The day before, an ugly, mostly unreliable junker sat in that same parking spot, but now it was gone. For the first time in ten years, I had a nice car again.

The past decade had been hard. By age twenty-six, I had become a millionaire. By age twenty-eight, I was bankrupt. I spent several years after that learning everything I could about how to handle money God's ways. I didn't just want to rebuild my former wealth; I wanted to honor God with that wealth. I had finally figured out that I was just a manager and God was the Owner, and I wanted a second chance at success. He had trusted me with a lot early on, and I had failed. I had shown Him—and myself—that I wasn't a good manager. But now things were different. I was passionate about doing things the right way the second time around. My wife, Sharon, and I vowed after bankruptcy to never borrow another dime. We worked like crazy to get out of debt and clear of the bankruptcy. We pinched pennies, cut coupons, and skipped vacations. I worked eighty hours a week while she was home taking care of three little kids. We clawed our way out of the mess using biblical principles for handling money, and God blessed us. Our new business began to grow. Life got a little better. We were able to breathe a little easier. And bit by bit we were building wealth again—but you wouldn't have known it by my old car.

During those years, I drove the cheapest cars I could. We had more important things to do than buy nice cars, and honestly, I had gotten used to driving junkers. Then one day, I was driving myself and one of my company's vice presidents to an event where I was supposed to speak, and the latest in my proud line of cheap cars broke down. There we were, standing in the parking lot of a gas station with steam pouring out from under the hood of the car. We looked through the trash, found an empty jug, and used it to pour water into the radiator to cool down the car so we could get to the event. By that time, my net worth was well over $1 million again, so this whole scene was ridiculous. My VP chided me, saying, "You seriously have to get a better car. This is crazy! You have the money!" And he was right. The moment had arrived. I was way overdue for a nicer car.

I shopped all over for a great buy, and I finally found a great deal on a two-year-old Jaguar. That was kind of cool because I drove a Jag right before I went broke. It felt like God was saying He was restoring what the locusts had eaten.[1] So there

I stood in the parking lot of my office just looking at it. You'd think everything about that moment would have been perfect, right? I mean, I had done everything right this time. We had zero debt. I *owned* that car free and clear, and it was a perfectly reasonable purchase for my family. In a way, it represented a new way of life because it was a physical symbol that God's ways work—that I could build wealth again the *right way*. But as I stood there, I wasn't thinking of any of that. Instead, I suddenly questioned my decision. With the sunlight shining off this beautiful car, the only question that came to mind was, *Did I do something wrong?*

I started thinking about all the hungry children in the world, and I wondered what they'd think of my new car. How many kids could I have fed with the check I had just written? Then I started to worry about what my friends and customers and clients would say. Would they think I was a phony because I talked so much about generosity but I decided to spend this money on something nice for myself? Standing in the parking lot that day, I realized something. God had been teaching me about *money* for the past ten years, but now it was time for Him to teach me about *wealth*. Now, in *The Legacy Journey*, I want to share with you what I've learned.

But let's be clear right up front. I'll go ahead and ruin the end of the story for you. I didn't do anything wrong by buying that car. I think God smiled at me as I wrote that check. Depending on who you listen to or what you read about wealth, that may shock you. If so, then get ready to be shocked *a lot* in this book. It's time to see what God's Word really says about wealth. And trust me: It's a much different message than you're hearing in our culture today.

THE STORY SO FAR

You probably know my story. I've told it a zillion times on the radio, in books, and in my nine-week class, *Financial Peace University* (FPU). I hate repeating my story for those who already know it, but let me give you the short version just so you know where I'm coming from. I started out with nothing and became a millionaire by the time I was twenty-six. But my entire net worth was supported by a huge pile of debt. One bank called one loan early, and that started a domino effect of me losing everything I owned over the course of two and a half years. Then, with a toddler, a new baby, and a marriage hanging on by a thread, Sharon and I threw up the white flag and declared bankruptcy.

Wake Up!

As we went through those hard times of losing everything, God started showing us the basic principles for how to handle money in His Word: Get out of debt. Live on a budget. Live on less than you make. Save. Invest. Never cosign. Always get the counsel of your spouse. I discovered these fundamental tenets—the core things you do to win with money—straight out of Scripture. But because I was a young hotshot with all these letters and licenses after my name that said I'm supposed to know something about money, all of this was new to me and kind of jolted my system. God had used my financial crash to say to me, "Wake up, stupid! You're going the wrong way! What you're doing isn't in line with Scripture. It isn't even in line with common sense!"

I've talked with tens of thousands of families who have

gone through FPU who have had the same experience. When they learned these principles for the first time, it felt like God was grabbing them by the shoulders and saying, "Wake up!" That's what FPU and my books *Financial Peace* and *The Total Money Makeover* have been about. Their purpose is to get you to that wake-up, then moment—that point where God gets your attention and you start to turn your financial life around.

So if *Financial Peace* and *The Total Money Makeover* are about waking up, *The Legacy Journey* is about growing up. At some point we all have to move beyond just drinking milk and learn to eat solid food. We must mature in our view of wealth. That means we have to emotionally and spiritually grasp wealth as a concept through the lens of Scripture. As we do that, our perspective changes. We really start to take hold of our role as managers—stewards—of the resources God has placed in our hands. What you do with His resources is what your legacy is all about.

What's the Problem?

Here's the problem: God's ways of handling money actually work. If you do the things I teach from God's Word, if you are diligent and wise with your income, then over time you will become wealthy. No matter who you are or where you're starting from, you will at some point become one of those "rich people." I've seen it more times than I can count.

I was doing a book signing a while back and saw a guy in coveralls standing at the end of the line. Where I'm from, coveralls mean you do *real* work. You do the kind of work that's hard and dirty, so you put on the coveralls to keep your real clothes from getting ruined. This man waited patiently, but I could tell he was the kind of guy who didn't really like to stand around waiting. He had a head full of bushy gray hair and a matching gray beard. He looked tired too; it was easy to tell that he'd been on his feet all day. When he finally got to the book-signing table, I noticed that he didn't have a book in his hand. He was just holding a little scrap of paper.

He said, "Dave, I'm not here to buy your book." I thought, *Well, why would you want to stand in line for an hour just to tell me you didn't want to buy my book?* He continued, "I just want to tell you that I started listening to you on the radio ten years ago. I heard all those things you said about the Scriptures and I went and looked them up for myself, and I started living that way. And I gotta tell you, the stuff you teach on the radio works." Then he put that scrap of paper down on the table in front of me. There were two numbers written on it: -$66,283 and $847,623. I looked back up at him and saw this strong, burly workman with big tears in his eyes. He said, "The first number is where I started thirteen years ago, and the second number is where I am now. I started with a negative net worth and $66,283 in debt, and today I am debt-free with $847,623 in mutual funds. This stuff works, Dave."

That conversation meant so much to me that I kept that little scrap of paper. If you were to come visit me in my office, you'd see it in a frame on my bookshelf. I love it because it doesn't just represent a financial turnaround; it represents a total change of direction for an entire family. This guy's family going back several generations had never seen that much money before, but there it was. And because he taught his kids how to handle money, it would be there for them. And as it grew over time and his kids added to it, it would be there for his grandkids.

This one man applying God's ways of handling money—even with a modest income—had completely changed his family legacy. And that's the "problem" with handling money God's ways: You end up wealthy. So let's talk about that.

THE LEGACY JOURNEY FRAMEWORK

In my classes and other books, I explain in detail what I call the Baby Steps. This is the process for taking control of your money, getting out of debt, and starting your family on the road to financial security and long-term wealth building. I'm not going to reteach all of that here, but I will take just a second to review the seven Baby Steps:

Baby Step 1: Place $1,000 in a beginner emergency fund ($500 if your income is under $20,000 per year).

Baby Step 2: Pay off all debt except your home mortgage using the debt snowball.

Baby Step 3: Put three to six months of expenses into savings as a full emergency fund.

Baby Step 4: Invest 15 percent of your household income into Roth IRAs and pretax retirement plans.

Baby Step 5: Start college funding for your kids.

Baby Step 6: Pay off your home early.

Baby Step 7: Build wealth and give.

The first three Baby Steps are all about taking control of your money. In those steps, you're correcting bad behaviors, getting out of debt, putting some money in the bank, and basically cleaning up a mess. Those months or years can be tense, but they are crucial to changing your legacy. Once you hit Baby Step 4, though, you start to feel a different kind of tension. For maybe the first time, you're able to relax a little bit, take a breath, and realize that you're in a position to build wealth. And that's when you start facing the questions that popped into my head that day as I was looking at my new car. For this, there's a different process in place that works alongside the Baby Steps. I call it **NOW–THEN–US–THEM**, and it's the framework for your legacy journey.

NOW: Taking Control

When you first have that wake-up moment and start doing a budget and working through the Baby Steps, you are laser-focused on taking control of your money and cleaning up a financial mess. I call that stage the **NOW**. At that stage, you may be broke, behind on your bills, struggling to put food on the table, and always worried about making one paycheck last until the next one arrives. Picture it for a moment: You are at the kitchen table with your head down, slumped over a pile of bills. You can't look up, because there are about a dozen different crises right under your nose. All you're trying to do is take care of all the little fires going on *right now*. That's not a fun place to be, but that's where a lot of us start.

In the **NOW**, your job, first and foremost, is to take care of your family. The Bible says, "If anyone does not provide for his own, and especially for those of his household, he has denied the faith and is worse than an unbeliever" (1 Timothy 5:8). At this stage, if you are a believer, you should be tithing (giving a tenth of your income) to your church, but now is not the time to give extra beyond that. And you shouldn't feel guilty about that either, because you are obeying your biblical mandate to take care of your family. This is also not the time to invest or fund the kids' college accounts. The long-term plan is to completely change your family's legacy, but that may seem like a tiny dot on the horizon at this stage. In the **NOW**, the goal is to stop the bleeding and get your feet under you.

THEN: Getting a Future Focus

Getting through **NOW** may seem like an eternity because you are working so hard and feeling completely stressed out, but over time, you start to take control of things. As you keep moving through the Baby Steps, you start to relax and are able to breathe again. Finally, you start to get a little wiggle room. If you've already been through the **NOW**, you know exactly what I'm talking about. You might even remember a specific moment when you realized that things were changing. That's a great place to be because as soon as the pressure eases, you are able to lift your head up a bit. When that happens, you can take your eyes off the **NOW** and start focusing on the **THEN**.

The **THEN** stage challenges you to adopt a future focus. By this point, you should be at Baby Step 4, investing 15 percent of your income into retirement, and Baby Step 5, funding your kids' college accounts. You can even start attacking the mortgage to pay off the house early, which is Baby Step 6. That's a much different place mentally, spiritually, and emotionally than the **NOW**, isn't it? With **NOW**, you're just trying to make it through the end of the week, but in **THEN**, you're able to look out at the future you're working so hard to create for your family. Scripture says, "Where there is no vision, the people perish" (Proverbs 29:18 KJV). At this stage, you're getting a vision for where you're going, which is crucial to your long-term success.

US: Creating a Family Legacy

While you're working on **NOW** and **THEN**, you often have tunnel vision because you're so focused on getting your own finances and future under control. But once you start building some wealth in your mutual funds and 401(k), and as you get closer to finally paying off the mortgage, you start to realize that you really are going to retire with dignity. You're not ready to retire yet, but that tiny dot on the horizon has gotten bigger. It's coming into focus, and it doesn't feel like a daydream anymore. This is going to happen, and you're going to be fine.

Just breathe that in for a second. Imagine your family—your kids, your grandkids, and maybe even your future great-grandkids—taken care of for generations to come. I call this stage **US** because it's not just about you and your spouse anymore. The Bible says, "A good man leaves an inheritance to his children's children" (Proverbs 13:22). This isn't about getting out of a mess; this is about changing your family tree.

In the **US** stage, you're talking to your kids about money and making sure they have the emotional and spiritual maturity to manage the wealth you might leave them someday. You're also teaching them to build wealth themselves. And more than anything, you're making sure they're not confused about God's ownership and their role as manager of what He's provided.

If you're not intentional about growing your kids' characters and ability to handle money, you can work your whole life to build wealth only to have it end up ruining them. As you work through **US**, you're making sure that will never happen.

THEM: Leaving a Legacy for Others

As you get to the end of the legacy journey framework, you know that the bills are paid—that's **NOW**. You know that you're going to be able to retire with dignity and send your kids to college—that's **THEN**. You know that you are taking steps to prepare the next generation to carry your new family legacy forward—that's **US**. And then, finally, you see the big picture—the **THEM**.

The **THEM** stage represents all the needs in your community and around the world, and you begin to see how God can use you to meet some of those needs. Your vision expands and you start to see the world through Christ's eyes. Suddenly you see wells that need to be drilled in Haiti. You see the HIV prevention efforts in Africa. You see mosquito nets that can be used to prevent malaria. You see the hungry children right down the street. You see the broke, scared single mom at the other end of the pew who can't pay the light bill this week—and who might need a reliable car too. At this stage, you're able to open your eyes and see—maybe for the first time—how you can make a difference in the world.

Proverbs says, "He who gives to the poor will not lack, but he who hides his eyes will have many curses" (28:27). I don't think most of us ever actually hide our eyes; I just think the pressures we're under keep our heads down so we can't see. But as we work through these biblical principles about taking care of our family first, casting a vision for the future, and leaving an inheritance to our children's children, we're able to lift our heads and look clearly into the future. God can do amazing things through us in that future. But we have to take it one step at a time, first through **NOW**, then **THEN**, then **US**, and finally to **THEM**. And that's where we get to help change the world. That's a powerful legacy.

YOU ARE HERE

No matter where you are in the Baby Steps, *The Legacy Journey* will give you a clear, biblical view of wealth and generosity. You may not be financially ready to change the world today, but you need to see where God might take you one day. If you are just getting started, meaning you aren't living on a budget, you have some debt (including cars and student loans), and you have nothing in savings, then you really need to get those things under control. Use *Financial Peace University* or *The Total Money Makeover* to get started immediately. It's never too early—or too late! That's the foundation for everything in this book, and those are the resources and tools that will get you through **NOW** and **THEN**.

Most of all, at this point I want you to grasp that if you are diligent in handling God's money God's ways, you *will* walk through these steps of building wealth. So don't be surprised when, as you move out of debt, learn to live on less than you make, give, and save, you become wealthy. If you are diligent with the steps, your eyes will look up from the **NOW**. You will begin to look toward the future with the **THEN**. You will become concerned that the next generations of your family are set up in the **US** stage. And of course, once that is done, it will feel natural and easy to meet the needs that God sets before you in the **THEM**. This is a biblical process, so you are not doing anything wrong by first taking care of your family, then your future, then future generations of your family, then finally to be outrageously generous with the wealth that God has allowed you to manage for His glory. So if the world or toxic "Christian" voices are trying to send you on a guilt trip, take heart that you are walking through a biblical process.

The Legacy Journey is primarily designed for those of us in the later Baby Steps—Baby Step 4 and beyond—who are working on **US** and **THEM**. We're going to talk a lot about wealth as a concept, and we're going to address a lot of the toxic messages in our culture that tell us we should be ashamed of the success God's given us. We'll talk about how to figure out how much is "enough" for your family, and we'll identify key things that should be part of your estate plan. We'll talk about how to keep money from ruining your relationships and your kids. And of course, we'll talk about that incredible day when your hard work and faithfulness have paid off, when you've paid the price to win, when you've lived like no one else, and you're finally ready to live—and give—like no one else. This is going to be a wild ride, and it's not just going to change your life. It's not just going to change your family tree. It's going to show you how to live *and* leave a lasting legacy of excellence.

CHAPTER TWO

The War on Success

A couple of years ago, I had an unbelievable opportunity to spend time with a group of ten incredibly successful, insanely wealthy business leaders. These were rich folks—*really, really rich.* The minimum net worth represented in the room was half a billion dollars. They were all totally committed, sold-out Christians. In fact, these guys were meeting to discuss the different ways their families had given to kingdom work in the past year. It was kind of a counsel of Christian philanthropists, and they met to discuss different giving opportunities and to encourage each other. When they added it all up, these ten families had given more than $1 billion to different ministries and mission work in just that one year alone. And there I was, sitting in the middle of it. Talk about feeling like a wiener in a steakhouse!

After a day of hearing these amazing stories of radical generosity, the meeting wrapped and the group headed out to dinner. The guy who called the meeting—the wealthiest man in the room—said, "Hey Dave, would you ride with me?" Now this guy is worth $2.2 billion. He's a business genius, a great Christian man, a great husband and father, and exactly the kind of person I like hanging out with. I want to learn from these kind of people because I want to grow up to be one! So when he asked me to ride with him, I was *in*. "Oh, you bet. I'll ride with you. You drive, and I'll take notes the whole time. Let's go."

As we were walking out, he said, "Listen, before we get out there, I want to apologize for my car." Honestly, it caught me off guard. He didn't really strike me as the kind of guy who'd roll up to a meeting of billionaires driving a junker. I said, "Why apologize? Are you driving a beater? We can take my car if there's something wrong with yours."

He said, "No, it's not that. I actually just bought a new car. In fact, it's the nicest car I've ever owned."

I had an idea of what was going on, because, like I said in the previous chapter, I had been there myself. But I asked anyway, "Why would you be ashamed of that?"

He hung his head a little bit and replied, "Well, it's a *really* nice car." About that time, we walked up to his parking spot. He wasn't kidding. I was looking at a brand new Mercedes. I looked the thing up when I got home that night. It was a $130,000 car. It was *sweet*. But instead of being excited about it, he felt like he had to apologize for it.

Let me tell you a little about this guy. He's worth $2.2 billion. That year alone, he had personally given away around $500 million to Christian ministries and Christian work around the world. But, of course, you'd never hear about that in the news or a press release because he didn't do it for you. He doesn't care what you think. He did it because he's a passionate giver, not because he wants to impress anyone or make headlines. So that year, after giving away $500 million to kingdom work, he bought himself a nice $130,000 car.

Guess what happened? He started getting hate mail—from Christians. Now, I think "Christian hate mail" should be an oxymoron, but I've gotten enough of it myself to know that it's real. He got notes and emails telling him how wasteful and selfish he was. They said things like, "You should have used that money to drill more wells in Africa" or "I wonder how many starving children you could have saved with that $130,000." These strangers—none of whom, I'm sure, had ever seen $1 million, let alone $2.2 billion—crawled out of the woodwork to condemn his decision and question his faith just because he bought himself a nice car.

I have to be honest: That bugs me. It bothers me because I know this guy. I know his heart. He's a strong believer. He's a follower of Christ. He's applied God's ways of handling money, he's faithfully provided tremendous value to his customers, he's given hundreds of millions of dollars to others, and he has been richly blessed by God. To see him criticized for enjoying the blessings God's given him hurts me, but it's something I'm seeing more and more of in today's culture. There's a war on success happening in America today, and it's something we as believers need to talk about.

THE ROOT OF ALL EVIL?

Money is not the root of all evil. Let me say that again: Money is *not* the root of all evil. The Bible does not say that, no matter how often you've heard it. It's one of those things that people are sure is in Scripture, but they're wrong. It's like the saying "God helps those who help themselves." A recent study found that 82 percent of Americans believe that is pulled straight from the Bible![1] It's not. But wait; it gets worse. Writing for Christianity.com, Albert Mohler went through more findings:

> A Barna poll indicated that at least 12 percent of adults believe that Joan of Arc was Noah's wife. Another survey of graduating high school seniors revealed that over 50 percent thought that Sodom and Gomorrah were husband and wife. A considerable number of respondents to one poll indicated that the Sermon on the Mount was preached by Billy Graham. We are in big trouble.[2]

I wonder what the response would have been if this poll had asked people if "Money is the root of all evil" is a verse from the Bible. People get all these crazy ideas about what the Bible says, but they never take time to slow down and see what it *really* says. If you want to truly mature in your Christian walk, you've got to take the time to actually dig into Scripture and see what's true and what's not.

Gnostics in the Land

First Timothy 6:10 does not say that money is the root of all evil. It says, "For the *love* of money is *a* root of *all kinds* of evil" (emphasis added). It's not about money; it's about our attitude. God doesn't like it when we worship anything other than Him. He's a jealous God, and if our love of money (or family, or career, or hobbies, or . . . you fill in the blank) gets in the way of our relationship with Him, then we have a problem. He doesn't like that.

Nevertheless, there are loud voices in our culture today of people who are supposedly steeped in intelligence and research and who constantly beat the drum that money is evil. But this false teaching is nothing new. In fact, it dates back almost to the birth of the Christian church in the first century when a group of early believers strayed from the teachings of Jesus and became heretics. That is, they preached and taught a false doctrine that went against the Scriptures. Central to their beliefs was the notion that all physical things, including material possessions, were evil. This group was known as the Gnostics from the Greek word *gnosis*, which means "knowledge." For this group, the only purity was that which was spiritual. If something could be physically seen or touched, then it was unholy. Flash forward two thousand years, and you can still see Gnostics in the land trying to convince us that material things are inherently evil. So a good income, savings, investments, a nice car, a big house—they're all evil. It doesn't matter how much you give or how much good you do with your resources. It doesn't matter how closely and faithfully you've followed God's ways of handling money. Your wealth is evil, period. That's a form of gnosticism, and it's a dangerous, heretical lie. It was heresy in the first century, and it's heresy today.

Lessons from a Rabbi

If money itself—not the love of money—is evil, then logic would say that people who *have* money must be evil as well. That means we as a culture get to vilify people who have become successful. I mean, only a filthy, nasty, self-serving jerk would pursue wealth if money were inherently evil, right?

I have a good friend who is an orthodox Jewish rabbi. Rabbi Daniel Lapin wrote a book several years ago called *Thou Shall Prosper*, and in it he explores how and why Jewish people—a stark minority in America—have a disproportionate amount of wealth. He told me that only about 2 percent of the US population is Jewish, but about 25–30 percent of the Forbes 400 (the four hundred wealthiest people in America) are Jewish. How is that possible? Rabbi Lapin's book outlines "Ten Commandments for Making Money" according to his Jewish tradition, and the first one is the most important. If there is one Jewish attribute more directly responsible for Jewish success in business than any other, it is this one: Jewish tradition views a person's quest for profit and wealth to be inherently moral.

I can't overstate that point. Believing that making money is a selfish activity will undermine anyone's chances of success. This is a dangerous socioeconomic trend that's running wild in our culture today. It's dangerous because any time you vilify success, nobody wants to become successful because they don't want to get any of that "evil" money.

Guess What: You're Rich

There's a point where the "rich is wrong" folks run into a problem. You see, the average household income in America is right around $50,000. Let's say your household income is well below the average and you make $34,000 a year. If you're living in America and your household makes $34,000 a year, you are in the top 1 percent of income earners in the world.[3] Not too long ago, the news was full of marches and demonstrations of people raging against what they called "one-percenters," meaning the top income-earners in America. Well, guess what? If your household makes $34,000 a year, you're rich. Welcome to the global 1 percent.

Let's go a step further. If you have an annual household income of just $11,000, you are in the top 14 percent of income earners in the world.[4] Here in the US, you'd be well below the federal poverty line, but from a global perspective, you'd still be pretty well off. Don't get me wrong; I know how hard it is to get by on $11,000 a year. I don't want anybody to have to do that. But from a global perspective, America has some of the richest poor people on earth! If you've ever visited a third-world country where people live in huts or shanties, have no running water, and don't know where their next meal will come from, then you return home to running water, indoor plumbing, and cabinets with food in them, your perspective changes. You realize pretty quickly how wealthy you really are.

See how this whole "wealth is wrong" belief system starts to break down? Can $34,000 be a "humble" or "righteous" amount of money in the US *and* an "evil" or "greedy" amount of wealth globally at the same time? It just doesn't make sense. Now if you're reading this and your household income is $34,000, I know you probably don't feel rich. That's because here in America, we compare ourselves to people who are richer than we are. But globally, you're still in the top 1 percent. So when we as a culture look down on "those greedy rich people," we're creating a massive hypocrisy because the people saying these things are usually, from a broader perspective, rich people.

But being "rich"—however you define it from a global perspective—is okay! The Gnostics were heretics, remember? The

Bible never says that wealth is wrong in and of itself. In fact, the Bible encourages God's people to take control of money for kingdom work. Over and over again, we see stories and examples of godly men and women who did just that. Abraham, Job, David, Solomon, and Lydia were all portrayed as wealthy in Scripture, but their wealth is never held against them. In fact, Scripture shows us some incredible things they were able to do with their money. Being able to use hard-earned wealth for kingdom work is an amazing honor and blessing! We should be excited that God's given us that opportunity. My friend Craig Groeschel, who pastors one of the largest churches in America today, says, "Why is it that the only blessing of God that we apologize for is wealth?" It's a great question. I think part of the reason is that we often don't handle our money with the right spirit.

THREE SPIRITS OF WEALTH

When it comes right down to it, there are only three main spirits —or attitudes—you can have with wealth and possessions. I'll go ahead and tell you up front that two of them are wrong and one of them is right. I'll also tell you that I've been guilty of all three of them throughout my life, which means I've gotten it wrong more often than I'd like to admit. I first came across these three views in a book called *The Blessed Life* by my friend Robert Morris. Robert points out how Mary, Martha, and Judas react to Jesus in two specific encounters, Luke 10:38–42 and John 12:1–8. Let's look at those passages and examine what each of these three people said and did. If you're like me, you'll probably see yourself in at least one (but probably all) of these positions.

The First Spirit: Pride

> Now it happened as they went that He entered a certain
> village; and a certain woman named Martha welcomed
> Him into her house. And she had a sister called Mary,
> who also sat at Jesus' feet and heard His word. But Martha
> was distracted with much serving, and she approached
> Him and said, "Lord, do You not care that my sister has
> left me to serve alone? Therefore tell her to help me."
> And Jesus answered and said to her, "Martha, Martha,
> you are worried and troubled about many things. But
> one thing is needed, and Mary has chosen that good
> part, which will not be taken away from her." (Luke
> 10:38–42)

The first spirit of wealth is pride, which says money comes
from me. I did it. I worked hard and created the money all by
myself. I went out, killed something, drug it home, and now I
can do whatever I want with it. This is the spirit I fell into early
on, before I lost everything in my late twenties. It's also one
that's easy for me to fall back into from time to time, because
I believe in hard work.

That actually goes back several generations. The Ramsey
family has always been a hardworking bunch of people. We've
all had varying degrees of success, but we could outwork just
about anyone around. That's one of the biggest lessons I learned
from my parents. I remember once asking my dad for some
money so I could ride my bike down to the local gas station
and buy a Coke. He looked down at me and said, "You're twelve
years old. You don't need money; what you need is a job!" So
instead of a dollar, he gave me a lawnmower! Our family is

originally of Scottish descent, and several years ago I had the chance to visit Scotland where we found the Ramsey Castle. As we toured the place, I noticed this huge coat of arms hanging on the wall. Printed above the coat of arms were two words in Latin: *Ora et Labora*, which means "Pray and Work." For hundreds of years, the Ramseys have been known for those two things: prayer and work.

People with the spirit of pride believe that money only comes from hard work and force of will. These are performance-based individuals who believe their wealth (and maybe even their spiritual growth) is 100 percent tied to their effort. And again, I've spent a lot of time in this zone. People struggling with a prideful spirit about wealth like to quote the parts of the Bible that elevate hard work. We say things like, "If you don't work, you don't eat" (2 Thessalonians 3:10); "The diligent prosper" (Proverbs 13:4); "When you're faithful with a little, more is given to you to manage" (Luke 16:10); or "You reap what you sow" (Galatians 6:7).

I love verses like that. I believe in hard work, and I believe those passages exalt the need to work hard and to be diligent with the work God's given you to do. But I do not believe a farmer who is mature in his faith has any question about where the rain comes from. He can work the land, line up his crops, and plant the seed, but he knows all of that work is meaningless if God doesn't provide the rain. Ignoring God's role in our success is a dangerous place to be because it puts the full burden of the outcome on our shoulders—and our shoulders just aren't big enough.

That's the trap Martha falls into in Luke 10:38–42. Read the passage again. Martha is amazing! She's doing all the right things. She's giving Jesus her very best work. She's cooking and cleaning. She's getting the house ready. She's keeping everyone comfortable and fed. You can picture her running around with a pitcher of iced tea, making sure all the tea glasses stay full. She's working her tail off! I love Martha in this story because *I've been* Martha so many times. And I'll tell you something else: Our churches *need* people who get excited about working hard. There's nothing wrong with working hard. But here's the issue with Martha in this passage: Jesus, the Son of God, is sitting in her living room . . . *and she's running a vacuum!* She had the opportunity to spend time at Jesus' feet, and, instead, she's doing the dishes. I've done that! I've been so blinded by the work that I've totally missed the real blessing in a situation. That's what we do when we think that money or wealth or possessions or God's favor and blessings come only from our performance.

The Second Spirit: Poverty

Then, six days before the Passover, Jesus came to Bethany, where Lazarus was who had been dead, whom He had raised from the dead. There they made Him a supper; and Martha served, but Lazarus was one of those who sat at the table with Him. Then Mary took a pound of very costly oil of spikenard, anointed the feet of Jesus, and wiped His feet with her hair. And the house was filled with the fragrance of the oil. But one of His disciples, Judas Iscariot, Simon's son, who would betray Him, said, "Why was this fragrant oil not sold for three hundred denarii and given to the poor?" This he said, not that he cared for the poor, but because he was a thief, and had the money box; and he used to take what was put in it. But Jesus said, "Let her alone; she has kept this for the day of My burial. For the poor you have with you always, but Me you do not have always." (John 12:1–8)

The second spirit of wealth is poverty, which says that wealth and possessions are evil. There's that Gnostic influence again, right? People with the spirit of poverty can tell you all about what other people should do with their money. These are the people who would have sent hate mail to my friend in the opening of this chapter for buying himself a nice car. They like to say things like, "He shouldn't have bought that" or "He could have helped so many people with that money." It's like their goal is to make successful people feel guilty about their success.

Judas represents the spirit of poverty in John 12:1–8. Even though his real motive was to steal the money, he echoed the condemnation that's become so common in our own culture. "She *shouldn't* have . . ." "She *could* have . . ." "Why *didn't* she . . ." Poverty thinking is always focused on other people's money, and it often gets obsessively focused on an unbiblical notion of equality (which we'll discuss in more detail in the next chapter). If there are two people in a room, one rich and one broke, then a modern-day Robin Hood should come in, take the rich person's money, and give it to the broke person. The fact that Robin Hood was a thief isn't important.

But the spirit of poverty doesn't care how the rich person got rich and how the broke person got broke. The spirit of poverty shouts, "Equality! Spread the wealth! Give your fair share!" It wants to take from the rich and give to the poor, no questions asked. And if the rich person refuses, then he's branded a selfish jerk and comes under harsh public condemnation. I've watched that happen to a lot of my friends, and it's not pretty.

The Third Spirit: Gratitude

The third spirit of wealth is the proper response to wealth. The spirit of gratitude says wealth is *from* God and *belongs to* God. This is where I want to be and where I want to stay. This is where I pray you'll aspire to get to, as well. In John 12:1–8, which we just looked at, we see the spirit of gratitude in the actions of Mary. The spirit of gratitude knows that "the earth is the LORD's, and the fulness thereof" (Psalm 24:1 KJV). Psalm 50:10 says that He owns the cattle on a thousand hills. And guess what? He owns *the hills* too! He owns everything, and He asks you and me to manage it. It's not ours. We're just His managers.

The spirit of gratitude says *thank you*. Thank You for giving me the money to take care of my family and put food on the table. Thank You for the ability to buy a decent car and take my wife on a great vacation. Thank You for providing for my needs today and my retirement tomorrow. Thank You for Your principles on how to handle money because using them has allowed me to change my family tree and leave a legacy that will outlive me. At its core, the spirit of gratitude says, *God, I'm going to manage this wealth and this stuff Your way—because it's Yours. Thank You for trusting me to manage it for You.*

I love the John 12:1–8 passage because it shows how radically extravagant our gratitude can and should be. Let me help you with this. Judas is disgusted with Mary's sacrifice because she could have sold the perfume for three hundred denarii. Do you have any idea what that would mean in today's terms? Three hundred denarii would have been the equivalent of about one year's worth of wages. The average income in America today is right around $50,000. So, for some present-day perspective, it would have been like Mary pouring $50,000 worth of perfume on Jesus' feet! And this was the *good* stuff. My wife informed me a long time ago that cheap perfume isn't nearly as strong per ounce as the expensive ones. With the drugstore brands, you have to pour half the bottle on your neck. But the good stuff— all it takes is one drop, and it fills the room.

That's the picture here: Mary poured $50,000 of fine perfume on Jesus' feet. That smell wouldn't have just filled the room; it would have filled the street. The whole neighborhood must have known something special was going on. And Jesus made it perfectly clear that Mary wasn't just making an offering; she was anointing Him for His burial. Days later, when Peter and John burst into Jesus' tomb, what did they find? Well, I can tell you that Jesus' body wasn't there—but the sweet smell of that perfume probably was. In her extravagant spirit of gratitude, Mary didn't hold anything back. She was so overcome with gratefulness that she gave her very best to the Lord. I want to note, though, that Scripture doesn't tell us that she gave *everything* she had or that she walked away from that encounter completely broke. People like to make that assumption, but it's just not in the text. We'll actually deal with the "give it all away" mentality later in this book.

The Source of Gratitude

My daughter Rachel Cruze and I recently wrote a book together called *Smart Money Smart Kids*. While working on the chapter on contentment, we had a great discussion about where gratitude comes from. As we talked through it, we started to see a progression where people move toward gratitude and into contentment. I believe the start of that process is humility. When I talk about humility, don't misunderstand me. I don't mean humiliation. Humility and humiliation are two totally different things. Humiliation is about shame or embarrassment. Humility, though, is a right understanding of myself and my place in the world. It's the opposite of entitlement. Humility recognizes that God is 100 percent responsible for every blessing, every success, every outcome, and every reward in my life. I only have these things because God gave them to me. Sure, I worked hard, but God provided the result. Like Proverbs says, "The horse is made ready for the day of battle, but victory rests with the LORD" (21:31 NIV).

Humility, then, leads into gratitude. That's an understanding not only of ownership and the source of the blessing, but also of the price that was paid to provide that gift. A good friend of mine once told me about the bicycle he got one Christmas when he was a boy. He was at that age when all his friends started riding bikes everywhere, and he wanted one more than anything. It's all he asked for that Christmas. The problem was, though, that his parents were broke. These were hard-working people who were doing what it took to put food on the table and keep a roof over their heads. A bike under the Christmas tree was a big deal to this family. Unless something changed, it meant they wouldn't *eat* for a few weeks! But this guy's dad wanted to give his son a bike for Christmas, and so he worked. He worked like crazy. He worked nights, he took extra shifts, and he got a weekend job. He was completely focused on this goal. And so, as my friend told me the story of waking up to see that bicycle under the tree that Christmas morning, he teared up.

That was decades ago. My buddy is a grown man now with a family of his own. But remembering the price his father paid to buy that bike still chokes him up. And do you think that bike was ever left in the rain? Do you think it was ever left outside a store or school without a chain on it? Do you think it ever had half-empty tires or scratches on the paint? No way! Even as a boy, my friend recognized the true value of the gift, and in his gratitude, he treated that bike like his baby. That's the kind of gift that brings tears to a grown man's eyes, and that's the kind of bike that you find in your grandfather's attic because he never could dream of throwing it away. There's just too much sentimental value attached to it.

That's gratitude, and it's evident in the way we manage the gifts we've been given. When I have a spirit of gratitude—when I am faithful with the little things because I know I don't really own any of it—the strangest thing happens. God gives me more to manage. And the more He gives, the more convinced I am that I don't own it. Looking to the future, I've instructed my kids that they don't own it either. When I die, they'll take over the *management*, not the *ownership*—because it's not mine to leave them. Who's the true heir of my estate? It's the current owner: Jesus Christ. He owns it now, and He'll own it then. If my kids or grandkids ever get confused about that, then there are clearly defined corrections written into my estate plan. We'll cut them out of the will if necessary because I refuse to let anyone try to take ownership of what God's given me to manage.

This is how I show my gratitude. This is how I try to say *thank You*. It's my best shot at being like Mary because Lord knows I've been like Martha and Judas plenty of times. I've been the guy who got puffed up about what *I* accomplished through *my own* hard work. I've put my faith in my accomplishments. I've judged other people because they gave too much or didn't give enough. I've looked down on people for buying "too nice" a car or house. I've operated under the spirit of pride and the spirit of poverty more times than I'd like to admit, but with God's help, I'm moving out of those spirits for good. My goal now as I get older is to operate most often in the spirit of gratitude, where how I act and how I do business and what I say are all saying the same thing: *thank You*. That's what I want for you too.

Snares and Dares

O ver the past few years, I've really gotten into the whole social media thing. When Twitter first started, the "cool" people on my team tried to get me to create an account, but I laughed it off. Honestly, I just didn't get it. I've got more important things to do than to stop what I'm doing to tell the world what I ate for breakfast! Because back then, that's all you saw. Nobody really knew how to use the thing yet, so it was kind of a waste. Today is a totally different story, though. Once Twitter really got its legs under itself, it (and other social sites) completely changed how people interact with each other and with companies. For the first time in my career, I was able to have direct, one-on-one, back-and-forth, 140-character conversations with tens of thousands of people. It was awesome! I learned things about my audience that I never knew, and that part of it has been a blast! Twitter, Facebook, and the myriad of other social media sources give us instant polling of what is going on in the culture—what people are thinking—and that can be inspiring and/or really scary.

There's another side to social media, though, that's been equally eye-opening. Having a Twitter account meant that I was wide open to all kinds of people who just wanted to take shots at me or, worse, take shots at the biblical principles I teach. After a few years and a half-million followers (and counting), I think I've heard just about every anti-Christian, anti-Dave, and antiwealth comment you could imagine. A lot of it comes from people outside the church, and that's fine. I love hearing from people with different backgrounds and different perspectives. But a lot of it has come from fellow Christians—men and women who have honest disagreements with my take on things or who are coming at the whole idea of biblical wealth from a totally different angle. And honestly, I enjoy that too.

The dialogue I've been able to have with such a diverse audience is amazing, and it's shown me several key areas where people get confused when it comes to a biblical view of wealth. Some are honest disagreements and others are outright attacks on biblical principles, but the themes are important enough that I want to take a good look at the big ones. These are snares that keep tripping many of us up as we try to understand God's view of wealth and success. In fact, some of them are things that tripped me up too when I first started thinking through all of this. So let's take a look at the key snares and see how we can avoid them. Then, I'll follow that up by making some dares—laying out the practical steps that will serve as a roadmap for your legacy journey.

SPOTTING THE SNARES

Before we get into the big snares, we need to look at a couple of nonnegotiables. These are two things that we might take for granted if we're not careful, but that can derail our whole legacy. The first thing is your commitment to a regular monthly budget. I've always said that your number one wealth-building tool is your income. Get-rich-quick is a fairy tale 99.9 percent of the time. The real key to building wealth is diligently managing your income over a long period of time. That's why the budget is so important, and that's why I stress the need to do a zero-based budget so much in my other books and all through our *Financial Peace University* class. The budget is your blueprint; without it, the whole thing falls apart. Jesus said, "For which of you, intending to build a tower, does not sit down first and count the cost, whether he has enough to finish it—lest, after he has laid the foundation, and is not able to finish, all who see it begin to mock him, saying, 'This man began to build and was not able to finish'?" (Luke 14:28–30). The monthly budget is how you "count the cost" with your money. I know from experience and from walking with millions of people through the process that the fastest way to fail with your money is to skip the monthly budget.

That's why it's so weird to me when I hear people say things like, "I can't wait to be financially secure enough that I don't have to do a budget anymore." What? Let me clear something up for you: The moment you stop doing a monthly budget is the moment your wealth building will start to fall apart. I don't care how much wealth you have or how much money you make, you never outgrow the need to do a monthly budget. Even after all these years, you'd better believe that Dave and Sharon Ramsey sit down and do the budget every single month. This is the simplest but most important part of everything that we're trying to build here, so don't skip it. Ever.

Second, and this seems like a no-brainer, debt can never again be an option. The Bible says absolutely nothing positive about debt. Every time debt is mentioned, it comes with a warning or condemnation. Debt is a trap, and it will steal your legacy. The Bible says that the borrower is slave to the lender (Proverbs 22:7). You will never be so "sophisticated" that you can safely play around with debt. I've talked about that plenty in my other books and classes, so I won't go back into all of it here. Just don't do it, okay?

A Word of Warning

Wealth is powerful and, therefore, dangerous. It is not for the spiritually immature. In fact, wealth is so powerful that a significant portion of the Bible's teaching on wealth focuses on the dangers. As we look at some of the warnings and snares, we should learn to take caution—but this does not mean we are called to avoid wealth as if it were evil. Most of the toxic, antiwealth messages in today's culture come from people who see a warning to remain cautious and mistakenly turn it into a prohibition. When wealth is viewed incorrectly or handled wrong, it can be a tremendous spiritual problem, so beware. But avoiding it altogether isn't the solution. Money is a fact of life, and it's one of God's blessings, so let's learn how to handle it well.

Worship the Provider, Not the Provision

Sometimes people get confused about things when they finally have a little money. When you're broke and struggling, it may be easy to trust God to meet your needs. You don't have any other choice! But once you start to build some wealth, it's easy to become distracted. If you're spiritually immature, a pile of money can turn into an idol, and you may try to draw security from it instead of from the One who gave you that money in the first place. Scripture says, "The name of the LORD is a fortified tower; the righteous run to it and are safe. The wealth of the rich is their fortified city; they imagine it a wall too high to scale" (Proverbs 18:10–11 NIV). That is, the righteous run to God while the foolish trust their money. Proverbs 11:28 makes it even clearer: "He who trusts in his riches will fall, but the righteous will flourish like foliage."

Spiritually mature people, no matter how much wealth they do or don't have, understand that God is the Provider and money is the provision. You never want to fall into the trap of worshipping money. That's like getting an amazing gift from your parents on Christmas morning, but instead of thanking your parents, you thank the gift. It just doesn't make sense. The gift is an inanimate object; it doesn't have feelings or morals or intelligence. It's just a thing. Money is the same way. So throughout our whole legacy journey, we must always worship the Provider, not the method He uses to provide for us.

Wealth Comes from Work

I believe without a doubt that God is the Provider, and He's the source of every dollar I've ever made. But that doesn't mean I've just sat around waiting for God to knock on my door with a handful of hundreds. That's not how it works. Remember the motto on the Ramsey family crest? Pray and Work. I think that's what God expects from us. That's the kind of attitude and activity He can bless. God promises to feed the birds, but He doesn't throw worms into their nests. Colossians tells us to do our work "heartily, as to the Lord and not to men, knowing that from the Lord you will receive the reward of the inheritance; for you serve the Lord Christ" (3:23–24). Proverbs says, "Wealth gained by dishonesty will be diminished, but he who gathers by labor will increase" (13:11). Do you see the connection here? "He who gathers by labor" (the guy who works hard) "will increase" (will build wealth). So wealth is a result of faithful, diligent, hard work along with biblical management of that income. If you're not interested in working hard, you aren't interested in building wealth. More importantly, you are missing that work is part of the mature believer's spiritual walk.

Wealth Requires Maturity

Wealth can be deceptive. If you're not careful, it can change how you see yourself, other people, and everything around you. It can make you think that you're a bigger deal than you are. Wealth has a way of blinding people and making them forget what it took to get there. We've already talked about the passage that says the love of money is a root of all kinds of evil, but let's take another look at those two verses in a different light. First Timothy 6:9–10 says, "Those who want to get rich fall into temptation and a trap and into many foolish and harmful desires that plunge people into ruin and destruction. For the love of money is a root of all kinds of evil. Some people, eager for money, have wandered from the faith and pierced themselves with many griefs" (NIV).

Have you ever watched a cat chase a laser pointer? It's hysterical. If you put a little red dot of light in front of a cat, he will chase that dot around the floor, over furniture, and up the wall like he's lost his mind. It's like the whole world fades away and this insane animal only sees that one tiny target. That's how the Bible describes someone whose only goal is to get rich. You'll be blind to other people, you'll ignore needs around you, you'll neglect your family, and you'll do really stupid things with the money you have on the off chance of getting rich quick. Don't get me wrong; if you follow God's ways of handling money, you will build wealth. That's great, but the goal should never be wealth for wealth's sake. That's a petty, immature, self-centered attitude, and it's a trap for many people. Wealth demands maturity. Don't let wealth lead to laziness in your walk with God and indifference in your relationships with others. If you don't hold yourself to an ultrahigh standard, money will cause you to walk with a spiritual limp your whole life.

Wealth Is Uncertain

No matter how careful you are or how detailed your financial plan may be, you can never, ever put your faith in wealth. Even with the most careful planning, wealth is uncertain—but God's provision is constant. You can count on God; you can't count on the stock market. Amen?

You can be wise with your budgeting, saving, real estate, and investments, but you just can't count on the economy. When you put all your faith in your stuff, your stuff becomes an idol. Like we just talked about, you start worshipping the provision, not the Provider. Money is not designed to be worshipped; it's just a tool. If a fine craftsman hand-built you a beautiful piece of furniture, would you thank the craftsman or the tools he used to build it? That sounds silly, but when we put our faith in money, it's the same as thanking a screwdriver for our new cabinets. It just doesn't make sense!

In 1 Timothy 6:17, Paul tells Timothy, his young apprentice, "Command those who are rich in this present age not to be haughty, nor to trust in uncertain riches but in the living God, who gives us richly all things to enjoy." I love that verse for several reasons. First, despite what anyone says about the "evils" of wealth, this verse doesn't give any hint that wealth is wrong. It simply states that there are wealthy people in the world, and then it instructs them not to be stuck-up, greedy, arrogant jerks. Second, it makes it clear that you can't put your faith in "uncertain riches." If you don't think riches are uncertain, think about someone who loses millions in the stock market just because he bet his whole fortune on one single company's stock. He was a millionaire one day and broke the next. Can you say Enron? Or what about saving up to buy a brand-new, shiny car that you probably love a little too much, then parking at the mall and watching some kid bounce his mom's van door off your car? That dent's a good reminder of how "uncertain" riches can be.

Riches are fine, but you will not be taking them with you. I have never seen a Ryder truck following a hearse. You can't trust in "uncertain riches," but you can completely trust the living God. Third—and this is awesome—where does Paul say wealth comes from? It's right there: "God, who gives us richly all things." How about that? If wealth is so evil, why does God give it so richly? And for what purpose does He give us richly all things? So we can *enjoy* them. Isn't that interesting?

What's even more interesting is where this passage falls in Scripture—just seven verses away from the "root of all kinds of evil" verse that so many people use to prove that wealth is morally wrong. This is part of the *same discussion!* When you take one little step back and look at the context of the passage, it doesn't make sense to say that riches are evil in and of themselves, because if you read just seven more verses, you see that God is the One who gives us riches, and He gives them to us so that we can *enjoy* them! And if you read one more verse ahead to 1 Timothy 6:18, you see how much good wealth can do in the world when the wealthy are "rich in good works, ready to give, willing to share."

Yes, wealth is uncertain, but God is not. God is a rock. He's steady and secure. You can trust Him to hold your wealth because He's the One who gave it to you in the first place. Trying to nitpick and micromanage every single economic variable is a recipe for disappointment. We have to be faithful and wise, but we can't *control* the things that are *out of our control.* I like how Martin Luther said it: "I have held many things in my hands, and I have lost them all; but whatever I have placed in God's hands, that I still possess."

Wealth Equality Is a Myth

There is a rising tide of popular thought in our culture today that says everyone's wealth should be equal. We hear all about the one-percenters and the ninety-nine-percenters; the haves and the have-nots; Wall Street and Main Street; the rich and the poor. We even hear this in many churches, with well-meaning

Christians trying to figure out how to get everyone on equal ground. The problem is, Scripture doesn't teach that. Even Jesus said that we'd always have the poor with us (Matthew 26:11). So why do some argue that everyone's wealth should be equal across the board if even Jesus said it wouldn't be the case? Now, don't misunderstand me. I don't think Jesus meant that it's a *good thing* that the poor will always be with us. I don't want anyone to struggle. But at the same time, I don't for one second think that striving for some kind of forced wealth equality is at all biblical or even moral.

Probably the most telling passage to me in the whole discussion of wealth equality is The Parable of the Talents in Matthew 25:14–30. Jesus tells the story of a rich man who went out of town for an extended trip, and he left three servants in charge of different portions of his wealth while he was gone. In the parable, the master gave one servant five talents, another servant two talents, and a third servant one talent. In today's terms, a talent is the equivalent of about $500,000, so we're talking about some serious wealth here.

When the master returned, he found that the servants with two and five talents each doubled their money by making wise investments. But the servant with one talent had a different story. He was afraid of his master, so he just dug a hole and hid the money. He didn't lose any, but he also didn't make any. It was a total wash, and the master lost any opportunity for growth on that money while he was away.

What did the master say to this guy? He called him a "wicked and lazy servant." This servant was a horrible manager. The master knew from then on that he couldn't trust this servant with anything, because the servant was too lazy or scared to act. He just dug a hole in the dirt and hid the money. And the master's response was completely counter to what we're seeing in our culture today. He didn't feel sorry for the servant. He didn't take money from the two other servants who had doubled their wealth so he could give a little to the third. No, he actually did the opposite. He took the one talent—half a million dollars—away from the third servant and gave it to the guy with ten times more! It's almost backward from what our culture thinks as just these days. He took it from the poor guy and gave it to the rich one. This is a story that Jesus is telling? And the hero of the story is the one who was more faithful in his management of God's stuff and built more wealth? That's kind of weird in our culture, isn't it?

Now I know this parable isn't just about money. You don't need to email me telling me I've missed the point of the whole thing. But one of the major points in this story for me is that fair doesn't always mean equal in the Bible. I believe in a fair playing field and equal opportunity (which all three of these servants had), but I don't believe there will ever be equal results. What matters is being grateful for what we're given, taking responsibility for it, and then managing it well. Talent, looks, initiative, and intelligence are not distributed equally and neither is wealth. I can't play a guitar like Brad Paisley, I can't play golf like Tiger Woods, I am not a computer genius like Bill Gates, and almost all of you have better hair than I do, so there will be different economic results. We all have equal value before the Lord and are equal as humans, but we do not all bring the same level of economic service to the marketplace. Service to the marketplace generates wealth, not your inherent value as a human. I often hear Christians say things like "no one should be paid $100 million to throw a football." Why not? If Peyton Manning generates ticket sales, TV ratings, and fans buying NFL apparel more than you do, he should be paid more than you get paid. That is biblical. If you disagree, go read The Parable of the Talents again.

Can the Rich Go to Heaven?

It seems like every time I talk about the subject of biblical wealth, at least one person uses the story of the rich young ruler to prove me wrong. "Have you not heard, Dave, that rich people are not going to heaven? It says it right here. It's easier for a camel to go through the eye of a needle than for a rich man to enter the kingdom of God! Your wealth is going to send you straight to hell!" I have heard that message preached at me a thousand times, usually by people who don't know any other verse in the whole Bible. They throw this verse out there as a gotcha—like they've found the key to undermine the idea of biblical wealth building. Sadly, they have no idea what that passage is all about. In fact, I think Luke 18:18–27 may be one of the most-often-misinterpreted passages in the whole Bible, so let's take a look at what it *really* says.

This is how you usually see it quoted by the antiwealth crowd:

> Now a certain ruler asked Him, saying, "Good Teacher, what shall I do to inherit eternal life?" So Jesus said to him, "Why do you call Me good? No one is good but One, that is, God. You know the commandments: 'Do not commit adultery,' 'Do not murder,' 'Do not steal,' 'Do not bear false witness,' 'Honor your father and your

mother.'" And he said, "All these things I have kept from my youth." So when Jesus heard these things, He said to him, "You still lack one thing. Sell all that you have and distribute to the poor, and you will have treasure in heaven; and come, follow Me." But when he heard this, he became very sorrowful, for he was very rich. And when Jesus saw that he became very sorrowful, He said, "How hard it is for those who have riches to enter the kingdom of God! For it is easier for a camel to go through the eye of a needle than for a rich man to enter the kingdom of God." (Luke 18:18–25)

That sounds pretty clear, doesn't it? Here's a powerful, wealthy guy who asks Jesus how he can have eternal life, and Jesus tells him to go follow all the commandments. That alone is impossible. No one can keep all the commandments perfectly. But that doesn't faze this guy. He says, "All these things I have kept from my youth," meaning he is a conscientious, rule-following kind of person. He basically said, "Yeah, yeah, Jesus. I got that. No problem there. What else?"

Jesus is so wise. He sees straight through to the heart of this person. He knows this young man is looking for a checklist of things to do to make it into heaven, but Jesus won't play that game. Instead, He immediately calls out the one thing He knows will be a stumbling block for this guy: his wealth. And when the rich guy goes away sad, Jesus gives what many take as a condemnation against wealth in general: "How hard it is for those who have riches to enter the kingdom of God! For it is easier for a camel to go through the eye of a needle than for a rich man to enter the kingdom of God" (Luke 18:24–25).

45

Here's the problem: Most people stop reading the passage right there. They say, "Well there it is, Dave. It couldn't be clearer!" But if you stop at verse 25, you're missing the whole point of the passage. If you take it just two verses further, you see the true heart of the passage. When Jesus makes that bold statement in verse 25, saying how hard it is for the rich to enter the kingdom of God, the crowd is shocked. They reply in verse 26, "Who then can be saved?" You see, in those days, wealth was actually seen as a way to enter into the kingdom. Some thought you could buy your way in, and others thought that wealth was a sure sign of God's favor, so the wealthy were *obviously* bound for heaven, right? So when Jesus says how hard it is for the rich to enter the kingdom, the crowd is dumbfounded. They basically say, "Wait a minute. If even the rich—who obviously have God's favor and who can afford whatever sacrifice it takes to get right with God—can't get into heaven, what chance do any of us have?" It's not a condemnation of wealth; it's a desperate plea for help.

How does Jesus answer their question: If even the wealthy can't be saved, what chance do any of us have? He says, "The things which are impossible with men are possible with God" (Luke 18:27). Surprise! This passage isn't about wealth at all. Jesus wasn't proclaiming a doctrine on money; He was illustrating a powerful teaching about grace. Money doesn't do anything to impact your salvation. It doesn't get you into heaven, and it doesn't keep you out of heaven. There's only one way to heaven, and that's through Jesus Christ. That's what Jesus is saying: Salvation would be impossible if it was left up to us, but it isn't. Our salvation is entirely in God's hands, and He alone makes the impossible possible.

The point of this passage is that no one can go to heaven without Jesus. Murderers can't get there. Drug addicts can't get there. Prostitutes can't get there. Gossips can't get there. The rich can't get there, and the poor can't get there. We are all sinners, and none of us can get there except through Jesus. It would be, as Jesus Himself said, impossible. So to say that the rich can't get into heaven because of their wealth is actually a form of heresy. When someone says that, they are essentially saying that the sacrifice of Christ on the cross is not enough to provide salvation to someone who has too many zeroes on their balance sheet.

Let's push it just a little bit further. Remember, when Luke sat down to write his gospel, he didn't put in all the chapter breaks and neat little subheads that we see in our Bibles today. It was just a continuous narrative. And only sixteen verses after Jesus' encounter with the rich young ruler, Luke introduces us to another rich guy, Zacchaeus, at the start of chapter 19. Remember him? He was a wee little man, and a wee little man was he. What do we know about Zacchaeus? Well, I can think of three things: He was a tax collector, he was rich, and he was short. This is a perfect counterstory to the Rich Young Ruler, because it tells us flat out that Zacchaeus had ripped people off by breaking the commandments (Luke 19:8). Compare that to the rich young ruler who said he'd never broken a commandment since he was a boy! So we have two rich guys, one who kept the commandments and one who didn't. Guess which one came to Christ? It was Zacchaeus, the crook! How is that possible? Because "the things which are impossible with men are possible with God" (Luke 18:27). The point of these stories is that salvation comes through Jesus, not through your money—and certainly not *in spite* of your money.

Giving Until It Hurts

Luke is on a roll in his gospel, showing Jesus interacting with all sorts of wealthy people, teaching about money, and using money as a way to teach deeper spiritual truths. We've already talked about the rich young ruler in Luke 18, then we saw Zacchaeus in Luke 19, and that brings us to Luke 20–21. Here we find a story that's traditionally known as the Widow's Mite. The story as we usually hear it picks up in Luke 21:1–4:

> And He looked up and saw the rich putting their gifts into the treasury, and He saw also a certain poor widow putting in two mites. So He said, "Truly I say to you that this poor widow has put in more than all; for all these out of their abundance have put in offerings for God, but she out of her poverty put in all the livelihood that she had."

I have heard dozens of sermons preached on that passage, and most of them usually give the same message: *You've got to give sacrificially. You've got to give until it hurts. You've got to give like the widow, who put every dime in the offering. When the rich give out of their abundance, it's no big deal. But when you give it all, just like the widow, you really put your faith in God and trust Him for the blessing. Your heart should be just like the widow's who gave all she had.* If you've been in church for a while, I bet you've heard that sermon too.

This may be exactly what God meant when He inspired

Luke to put this in his gospel. It's a fantastic point, and it's a great picture of giving. However, something about that interpretation has always bothered me. All through the Bible, we see examples of sincere, generous, godly men and women who have wealth and are never condemned or criticized for it. We are instructed that we don't actually own anything; we are just managers. We've already seen that Jesus' call to the rich young ruler wasn't a teaching on giving away everything; it was a spotlight on that one person's idolatry and an opportunity to explain the doctrine of grace. Instead, the Bible says the diligent prosper (Proverbs 21:5); that in the house of the wise are stores of choice food and oil (Proverbs 21:20); that if you don't take care of your own household, you're worse than an unbeliever (1 Timothy 5:8); that a good man leaves an inheritance for his children's children (Proverbs 13:22). That's the consistent message of Scripture: We are called to faithfully manage His resources and take care of our family. Sure, that means we should be constant, consistent givers. Giving should always be part of your financial plan, no matter where you are in the process. I've talked a lot about that in my other books and classes, and we'll talk more about it later in this book. But in this passage, we don't see someone giving *a lot*; we see someone giving *everything* she had. The NIV translates it like this: "She out of her poverty put in all she had to live on" (Luke 21:4 NIV). Does that mean God wants us to stay in poverty and endanger our families? I don't think so. We have to ask what else may be going on here.

The first words out of Jesus' mouth in the passage may give us a clue. Like I said, most of the time when I've heard the Widow's Mite preached, the Scripture reading starts with Luke 21:1, "And He looked up and saw the rich putting their gifts into the treasury." Something about that feels weird to me. It feels like it's picking up in the middle of something, not starting a new story. Remember, Luke didn't break his gospel up by chapters and verses; that happened later. So if we ignore the chapter break between Luke 20 and 21 and look at the greater context of what Jesus was doing when "He looked up," the whole thing starts to look a little different. Let's back up just three verses to get a better sense of the context, and we'll run right through the Widow's Mite passage we looked at above:

> Then, in the hearing of all the people, He said to His disciples, "Beware of the scribes, who desire to go around in long robes, love greetings in the market-places, the best seats in the synagogues, and the best places at feasts, who devour widows' houses, and for a pretense make long prayers. These will receive greater condemnation." And He looked up and saw the rich putting their gifts into the treasury, and He saw also a certain poor widow putting in two mites. So He said, "Truly I say to you that this poor widow has put in more than all; for all these out of their abundance have put in offerings for God, but she out of her poverty put in all the livelihood that she had." (Luke 20:45–21:4)

Did you see it? Jesus condemns the religious leaders of that community. He calls them out for their hypocrisy, and He makes it clear to everyone around that those particular leaders just want to put on a show so people will think they're powerful and important. They make long, elaborate prayers so others will see how "spiritual" they are, and they always sit up front in the synagogue. They're *really* special. At least that's what they want everyone to think. You know what else Jesus condemns them for? Devouring widows' houses. Jesus is commenting on a religious system that these leaders have put in place that is actively harming the poor and the weak. He says they not only take the best seats at the feast, but they go a step further to *devour* widows' houses. They completely consume everything and everyone around them, including the weakest, most-struggling members of the community.

So if you ignore the chapter break, you see He *just* made that comment about devouring widows' houses, and *immediately* the passage continues, "And He looked up." What did He see when He looked up? He saw a poor widow putting *everything she had to live on* into the scribes' treasury. We always talk about the Widow's Mite as a story of giving sacrificially out of a good heart, but isn't it interesting that Jesus never says anything about the woman's heart? It doesn't say that she gave "out of love" or "out of a generous spirit." The passage says that she gave "out of her poverty." We can make all kinds of assumptions about her spirit, but this story takes place in the context of Jesus' condemning a religious system for stealing from the poor—and particularly a widow.

Those who think wealth is evil and believe the only moral thing to do with money is to give it all away love the story of the Widow's Mite. And honestly, the traditional take on this story may be right. I'm not a biblical scholar; I'm just a guy who's studied the financial teachings in the Bible to try to understand God's ways of handling money. But when I look at this passage in this context, it's hard for me to believe that God's using this one, probably victimized, lady as a model for giving.

Instead, I see it as a challenge for how the church should always strive to serve—not harm—its weakest members.

The stories of the Rich Young Ruler, Zacchaeus, and the Widow's Mite have been taught the same way for so long that it may be really uncomfortable to step back and look at them with fresh eyes. I get that. And I'm not saying that everything you've ever heard is wrong or that everything I'm saying here is right. But what I hope you'll do with these passages—and the whole Bible, for that matter—is to not take these amazing stories for granted. Dig in for yourself, read the passages, read what happened immediately before and immediately after each passage, and study commentaries. Don't get caught up in the chapter breaks and verse numbers that were added centuries later. And be very careful not to let your politics set you up to misinterpret Scripture. Use the power of the Holy Spirit and the brain God gave you to examine for yourself what message we're supposed to get from these passages. Then use that knowledge, guidance, and insight to avoid all the snares the Enemy has put in our way regarding wealth.

TAKING THE DARE

My friend and former pastor Dan Scott says, "Adults are asked to manage dangerous things well for the glory of God. Children are not." And guess what? Money is dangerous. It's not evil; remember, it doesn't have morals. But it *is* and *can be* dangerous. I've used the brick analogy in the past: Money is like a brick. You can use it to build a church, or you can throw it through a church window. The brick doesn't care what you do with it.

It can be a helpful tool, or it can be a weapon. To some degree, money is the same way. It is a responsibility that God's entrusted to us. With that in mind, I want to talk about what it means to accept that responsibility—or daring to win with money.

It's Okay to Enjoy Wealth

Much of the toxic teaching about wealth is the result of spiritual immaturity. Some people are hit with the "money is evil" message so hard that they honestly feel guilty if they start to win. That's a trap! If money were evil, then why would God's Word contain so many examples of incredible, faithful men and women who have massive wealth and yet whose devotion to God is never questioned? Abraham, Isaac, Jacob, Joseph, Job, David, Solomon, Joseph of Arimathea, and Lydia are just a few examples of biblical heroes who honored God with the wealth He gave them.

The fifth and sixth chapters of Ecclesiastes contain some of the hardest, most sobering teachings about wealth in all of Scripture. Those passages make it clear that wealth is a responsibility, and it's easy for that responsibility to lead some people off a spiritual (and financial) cliff. Like I said, money is dangerous, and if you see yourself as the owner instead of the manager, wealth will lead you into trouble every time. However, if you keep your perspective straight—if you are always aware of the fact that you're just a steward of what God owns—then you have every right to enjoy the blessings and benefits of that gift.

Now, because I told you to always keep the broader biblical context in mind, let's look at Ecclesiastes for a minute. Tradition says that it was written by King Solomon in his old age. What do we know about Solomon? I can think of two things right off the bat. First, God blessed him with wisdom beyond what had ever been known before. Second, Solomon was probably the wealthiest person in history up to that point. So, God gave him wisdom, and God gave him wealth. Wisdom *and* wealth. That's a pretty powerful combination. Of course, Solomon made mistakes. His wisdom and obedience to God were imperfect at times—after all, he was human. By the time he wrote Ecclesiastes, he had been through major ups and downs in his spiritual, personal, emotional, and financial life. He had seen it all, and at this point, he's ready to talk about it. So what does he say?

He spends most of chapter 5 warning us about the dangers of wealth and greed, which some use to support the "wealth is evil" belief. But, at the end of a rant against the misuse of wealth, Solomon pulls back and makes this observation:

> Here is what I have seen: It is good and fitting for one to eat and drink, and to enjoy the good of all his labor in which he toils under the sun all the days of his life which God gives him; for it is his heritage. As for every man to whom God has given riches and wealth, and given him power to eat of it, to receive his heritage and rejoice in his labor—this is the gift of God. (Ecclesiastes 5:18–19)

These two verses blow my mind! What is the focus of this message? It isn't me; it's not saying, "Look what I've done! I'm so awesome!" It isn't work; it's not saying, "My job is my provider." It isn't wealth; it's not saying, "Money is the goal, so go get you some." It isn't even the *enjoyment* of wealth or the different ways you can bless others with it. There is one and only one focus of these two verses: God.

This passage makes it perfectly clear. God is the One who gives us "all the days of [our] life." God gives us work. He gives us the energy and power to do the work. He gives us the "riches and wealth" that come from our work. And—don't miss this— He gives us the "power to eat of it" and "rejoice in [our] labor." It's all from God! The days, the work, the power to work, the reward from work, and even the *enjoyment* of the reward—the whole thing is His from start to finish! This is His gift to us, and it's not our *option* to enjoy it. Scripture says that it is our "heritage" to "enjoy the good of all [our] labor"!

God gives us these blessings to faithfully manage, and that means we should always be wise stewards. It means we should always be giving. It means we should always be taking care of our families. And yes, it means that we should actually enjoy the unbelievable blessings He has put in our hands! Spiritually mature people with a right view of God's ownership can do all of that. We don't have to be scared of the wealth or ashamed of the fact that wealth enables us to do some fun things. That's what my friend Dan Scott meant when he said, "Adults are called to manage dangerous things well for the glory of God." We're adults, and we're *managing* these things for God. According to Solomon, the wisest man who ever lived, part of managing our God-given wealth is honoring God with our enjoyment of that blessing.

I Dare You

The first purpose of this chapter is to give you some biblical warnings about the dangers of wealth, which we've called the snares. The second purpose is to show, based on God's Word, that good stewardship of God's resources includes building wealth for kingdom purposes and managing and growing that wealth. That's the dare.

Building wealth isn't for wimps. Being diligent in managing your income and actually building some wealth is hard work. Managing that wealth for the kingdom is harder. And so I dare you. I dare you to build wealth and use it as a tool to serve your family. I dare you to build wealth so you can retire with dignity. I dare you to build wealth so you can truly leave an inheritance to your children's children. I dare you to build wealth so you can change not only your family tree but also your whole community. I dare you to be a good steward because Scripture is clear that good stewards are given more to manage. The diligent are going to prosper, and that means if you really follow God's ways of handling money, you are going to build wealth. But that's not the goal. This is not about you; it's not about some hocus-pocus, pseudo-Christian formula so you can get rich. I'm not about you getting rich; I'm about God being rich and you managing it well for Him! So go out there and be successful—I dare you!

CHAPTER FOUR

The Law of Great Gain

After more than twenty years of doing financial coaching, working one-on-one with families, talking about money on the radio for three hours every day, writing books, doing research, and leading classes about money, I think I may have stumbled upon the most powerful financial principle that there is. I truly believe if you get this principle right, you can get out of debt. If you get it right, you can live on less than you make. If you get it right, you can save, invest, and change your family tree. If you get it right, you can build wealth, give, and make an enormous impact on the world for the kingdom of God.

But if you get this principle wrong, those same things will be affected negatively. You might stay in debt your whole life, always living paycheck to paycheck. You'd probably never have any savings for emergencies, and you would most likely never be able to build any wealth. You may never be able to retire with dignity—or retire *at all*, for that matter. You wouldn't have much to give, and you probably wouldn't leave much of an inheritance to your children's children.

Are you getting the idea that this is important? Does it sound like something that everyone on the planet, regardless of their level of wealth, income, or faith should pay attention to? Taking hold of this principle changes the shape, the speed, and the power of your legacy journey, but most people completely leave it out of their financial plan. But the truth is: I believe it is almost impossible to be successful without it. What's this big secret, this critically important financial principle? I'm talking about contentment.

UNDERSTANDING CONTENTMENT

People don't understand contentment today. In our materialistic, stuff-driven society, where bigger is better and faster is master, it can seem impossible to actually find contentment—to slow down and say, "I'm content with the car I have, the house I own, and the job I love." That doesn't mean we should stop setting goals and working toward them. We'll talk more about that in a minute. Instead, it's a spiritual exercise to stop in the middle of our go-go, frenetic culture and just . . . breathe. The Bible says it this way: "Now godliness with contentment is great gain" (1 Timothy 6:6). Whenever I see a phrase in Scripture like "great gain," I not only view it through a spiritual lens but I also view it through a financial lens. I think this is a financial principle. It's not about piling up stuff for the sake of stuff. It's not a prosperity message; it's a responsibility message. Our ability to build wealth, use wealth for the kingdom, and enjoy the wealth God gives us all boils down to whether or not we can keep that wealth in perspective. And that's a matter of contentment.

A Winning Attitude

What makes a bigger impact on your ability to win with money: your income or your attitude? Many people over the years have told me all about their debt and their inability to save, and they often say something like, "Dave, if I only made more money, then I could . . ." Well, sometimes that's true. Sometimes you really do just need to make a little more money. But more often than not, the problem isn't income; it's attitude. I can't tell you how many times I've talked to couples who say to me, "Dave, thank you for what you teach. We're doing so good. We have no debt and a full emergency fund. We've got $200,000 in our 401(k), and our kids' college is underway. Everything is awesome!" When I ask them what they make a year, they say $40,000. That's a great job.

But then I take two steps and someone else stops me. They'll say, "Dave, we need your help. We've got $50,000 in credit card debt. We owe $80,000 in student loans. We owe $30,000 on our car. We have no money in retirement and no savings for an emergency. Things are terrible!" Then I'll ask this couple how much they make, and they'll say something like $80,000. How is that possible? How can one couple be winning at $40,000 and another couple be losing—big time—at $80,000? The answer isn't math. If it were just about math, then the couple with twice the income should be doing twice as good, right? No, the problem is contentment. It really is the most powerful financial principle there is.

The Bible says, "Now godliness with contentment is great gain. For we brought nothing into this world, and it is certain we can carry nothing out. And having food and clothing, with these we shall be content" (1 Timothy 6:6–8). Contrary to some teaching, this passage is *not* saying that we should never have anything more than food, clothing, and basic necessities. The focus of this Scripture is not on the *stuff* but on the state of our spirit while we're in achievement mode. Contentment is not a lack of ambition or action or intensity. It's the condition of our hearts while we're pursuing those things. The question shouldn't be, "Is it okay for me to have some nice stuff?" The real question is, "If I *don't* have nice stuff, will my spirit be okay with that? Do I have to have this stuff in order to have peace?" If the answer to that last question is yes, then you may have a problem with discontentment.

See, content people don't always *have* the best of everything, but they always *make* the best of everything. Someone will always have a nicer car or a bigger house. Keeping up with the Joneses is a fool's game because someone always has something better. Besides, I've done detailed research into the matter, and guess what? The Joneses are broke! They're up to their eyeballs in debt just because they want to impress you. They don't have "great gain," because they're trying to fill a void in their hearts with *stuff.* Listen, don't get me wrong. I want you to have some nice stuff; I just don't want your nice stuff to have *you.* That's the problem we fall into when discontentment guides our actions. Keeping this spirit in check is an exercise in spiritual maturity that is critical to having a quality legacy journey. And it's an exercise you'll work through over and over and over again. You'll never "get there" when it comes to contentment.

That's because contentment is not a destination; it is a manner of traveling. It's not a place you're leaving from, and it's not a destination you're heading toward. It's how you're going about getting there. More than anything, it's how you feel in your spirit while you're making the trip.

Spiritual Jellyfish

Sometimes I hear people in the church say, "Well, if you were a content Christian, you'd be happy to just sit at home and pray all day. You wouldn't worry so much about working hard and making money. You'd just trust God to show up and take care of all your needs." That would make you a spiritual jellyfish, a blob just floating around with no backbone and no direction. That attitude comes from a total misunderstanding of what contentment really is. Nowhere in Scripture do we get the idea that contentment means apathy or lack of ambition. I see that "godliness with contentment is great gain" (1 Timothy 6:6), but I also see that I'm called to "do [my] work heartily, as for the Lord" (Colossians 3:23 NASB).

A contented spirit is never an excuse for idleness. Just look at the apostle Paul. This guy was super motivated and ambitious before he met Jesus, and he certainly didn't slow down after he met Jesus. This man had things to do, places to go, and people to see! He was *moving*. He never took his foot off the pedal no matter what he went through or what he was heading into. Instead, he said, "forgetting those things which are behind and reaching forward to those things which are ahead, I press toward the goal for the prize of the upward call of God in Christ Jesus" (Philippians 3:13–14).

Paul was always pressing. He was always moving forward.

He was always going somewhere and always had huge goals ahead of him. But isn't this the same guy who said, "I have learned to be content whatever the circumstances" (Philippians 4:11 NIV)? Sure it is. Paul didn't see a conflict between being content with what he had *and still* pressing forward. His contentment was not an excuse to sit around and do nothing. He knew God had big plans for his life, and those plans involved a whole lot of action. But Paul didn't *need* those plans to work out in order to maintain a peaceful spirit. In his heart, he was grateful for what he had, and that gratitude and contentment made him *more* excited—not less—to keep pushing forward into whatever God had in store for him.

Contentment doesn't mean I'm not going to set goals and try to reach them; it doesn't mean I'm going to sit back and relax and stop working at my career, relationships, and wealth building. But it does mean that I'm not going to be torn up inside with a lust for *stuff* while I'm working. I can be content, but I can still move forward.

UNDERSTANDING ENOUGH

The key question when it comes to contentment is "How much is enough for you?" That's a huge question, and it's a question that people will crawl out of the woodwork to answer for you. When you have a little wealth, it's amazing how many people will suddenly appear to tell you what you should do with it. More than that, though, they'll tell you what you *shouldn't* do with it. And too often, what they say you shouldn't do with it is enjoy it. Thank goodness it's none of their business.

How Big Is Your Chalice?

Back in Chapter 2, I mentioned my friend Rabbi Daniel Lapin and his book *Thou Shall Prosper*. Like I said before, that book had a huge impact on me because it makes such a clear, compelling case for the morality of building wealth—as long as you do it from an unselfish, nongreedy, biblical perspective. In his book, Rabbi Lapin lays out specific principles that Jewish people have used to win with money for thousands of years. Using those Old Testament principles as a lens, I've been able to look at the New Testament teachings with fresh eyes and see things I've never seen before. I've also discovered a whole new way to view the contentment issue—in an image that illustrates this more beautifully and clearly than anything I've ever seen. It's an ancient Jewish ceremony called the *Havdalah*, and Rabbi Lapin explains it this way:

> Jewish tradition strongly establishes the principle that each person makes his or her own needs the primary concern, although not the only concern. One could say that Judaism declares it necessary but insufficient to focus on one's own needs first. As the Sabbath ebbs away each Saturday night, Jewish families prepare for the productive work week ahead by singing the joyful *Havdalah* service. This observance divides the Sabbath from the upcoming work week and asks God to increase both the families' offspring and their wealth. It also highlights their hands, as if to beseech blessing on the work of those very hands. The *Havdalah* service is recited over a cup of wine that runs over into the saucer beneath.

This overflowing cup symbolizes the intention to produce during the week ahead not only sufficient to fill one's own cup, but also an excess that will allow overflow for the benefit of others. In other words, I am obliged to first fill my cup and then continue pouring as it were, so that I will have sufficient to give away to others.[1]

So you fill up your own cup first, which symbolizes taking care of your own household first (1 Timothy 5:8). That's what "enough" is for your family—whatever it takes to fill that cup. And then you keep pouring so you have plenty to give to others. I love this image. A pastor friend gave me a chalice and saucer years ago, so in some of my live events and video classes, I use that to demonstrate what it looks like to fill your own cup first. Once the wine reaches the lip of the cup, it flows over the top and down the sides of the chalice and fills the bowl. It's a beautiful thing to watch, especially if you see it as a metaphor for taking care of your own family and then the needs of other people.

But here's what I want you to understand about the *Havdalah* in light of this discussion on contentment: No one else can tell you how big your chalice should be. The size of your cup in this metaphor is 100 percent between you and God. There is no concrete, cookie-cutter answer for what "enough" looks like for every family. The top of the *Havdalah* cup doesn't have a dollar amount written on it that says you can have *this much* but no more. It's different for every family. A couple of hints though: First, if your family is lacking because of your extreme giving, then your cup might be too small. It isn't a thimble;

it's a cup. Second, if there is never any overflow to help others, then your cup might be too big. It isn't a swimming pool; it's a cup.

Only you and God can decide how much is enough for you. After all, He gave you this wealth in the first place. He is your loving Father who loves to give His children good gifts. He adores you, and He knows what's best for you. He can see where you'll be in twenty years, and He can see the impact of every decision you've ever made or will ever make. He holds your life in His nail-scarred hands. He gets to decide the size of your chalice—no one else.

The $100 Jeans Hypocrisy

Too often in our culture—yes, even our church culture—people around us try to play the role of the Holy Spirit by telling us how much is enough for us. The Pharisees and Gnostics are loose in the land, right? People pop up and say things like, "Her car is too expensive. No Christian should drive a car that nice." Or maybe, "Their house is entirely too big. They don't need that much space. What a waste of God's resources." Translation: "I have decided that your chalice is too big, and so I think you're a selfish jerk." Have you heard these messages? I've heard them my whole life, and I never knew what the measure was. But I think I've finally figured it out. Here's how it works for most people who spread these toxic messages: How nice a car is too nice? "A little nicer than the one I drive." How big a home is too big? "A little bigger than my home." If they can't even fathom ever owning something as nice as someone else, then that suddenly becomes the dividing line between holy and unholy. It's not based on Scripture, income, wealth, or anything like that.

It's based on each critic's twisted, limited, self-centered point of view. And that's just sad.

That's how you end up with billionaires, like my friend I told you about a couple of chapters ago, who can give away a half-billion dollars in a single year and yet still be criticized for buying a $130,000 car. Let me put that in perspective for you. This fine, successful Christian businessman is worth $2.2 billion. When you look at $130,000 in the context of $2.2 billion, it doesn't even show up. It doesn't move the needle at all. Him buying a $130,000 car is the financial equivalent of you and me buying a biscuit! It just doesn't matter to his financial situation at all. I guarantee you that most of the people who criticized my friend were spending a much greater percentage of their income on luxuries than he spent on that car.

But the modern Pharisees don't see it that way. Instead, these critics put on their $100 blue jeans, leave their nice homes, drive their SUVs to the trendy coffee shop down the street, pull out their $1,000 MacBooks, sip their $8 coffees, and type blog posts about how wealth is evil. And somehow, the way they do it is holy, but the way my friend (who gave away $500 million in a year) does it is unholy. It just doesn't make sense! It's like Judas complaining about Mary pouring out the expensive perfume (John 12:1–8). Besides, we've already seen that anyone making $34,000 in America today is in the top 1 percent of income earners worldwide. The size of your cup is relative to the size of your income, your family, and a million other variables. Ultimately, though, it's between you and God, and it is nobody else's business. Don't let anyone steal your enjoyment of the success God's given you. Remember, it's your heritage to enjoy it (Ecclesiastes 5:19).

DISCONTENTMENT DANGER SIGNS

What does it look like when we get confused about our role as manager and start thinking we're the owner? It gets ugly. Discontentment starts to grow in our hearts. It starts with just a little pinprick, but over time, that wound festers and gets infected until it's all about me. It's about what I want, what I can get, and what I think about what you have. We're going to look at a few signs that point to a problem with discontentment. I covered some of these briefly in my previous book, *Smart Money Smart Kids*, which I wrote with my daughter Rachel Cruze. That book looked at contentment from a parenting point of view. Here, I want to go a little deeper to see how discontentment impacts our character as we build wealth.

Attempting to Get Rich Quick

One sign of discontentment is attempting to get rich quick. You've seen these people, haven't you? They are always working some scheme, joining some weird investment group, and looking for a BBD—a bigger, better deal. They're basically dreaming of a lottery jackpot, and they'll throw thousands (or hundreds of thousands) of dollars into crackpot schemes thinking they've found a shortcut to wealth. Maybe they even want to share that "opportunity" with you—for a price. Let me burst that bubble: For 99.9999 percent of us, there is no shortcut. Sure, you could become wealthy very quickly if you invent the next Facebook (which took them years to build), but outside of that, get-rich-quick schemes are a fast track to losing all your money. Proverbs 28:20 says, "A faithful man will abound with blessings, but he who hastens to be rich will not go unpunished." Personally, I kind of like The Message translation of that verse a little better: "Committed and persistent work pays off; get-rich-quick schemes are ripoffs." Amen.

A bigger problem with trying to get rich quick, though, is that it represents a serious spiritual issue. God is the Owner, and He entrusts His wealth to us to manage. When you point all your guns at some crazy, overnight "wealth-building opportunity" that you saw on late-night cable TV or that your broke brother-in-law told you about, what are you really trying to do? Trick God into handing you more ahead of His schedule? Here's a thought: Maybe God knows how much you can handle right now and when you may be able to handle a little more. Most people don't have the emotional and spiritual maturity to go from broke to billions overnight. That's why you see so many horror stories of people whose lives are ruined within a couple of years of winning the lottery. When you drop a lot of money into a broken system, it just widens the cracks.

Trying to Appear Wealthy

The next sign of discontentment is trying to appear wealthy. There's a saying for that in Texas: big hat, no cattle. We all know people like this. These are the people who appear to have it all. They have a large, beautiful home with a perfectly manicured lawn. There are two brand-new luxury cars in the driveway. Their kids are in private school. They're always talking about some incredible vacation they just took. They have the nicest clothes, and their fingers and necks are dripping with diamonds. They look perfect, don't they? Well, more often than not, all of that is a façade that is hiding a mountain of debt, stress, and fear. That perfect couple may spend every night yelling at each other over the debt. They might be buying their groceries with their credit cards. They could be (and probably are) one missed paycheck away from losing everything. And it's all because they want to put on a show for the world, dressing their lives up in what looks like success but is really a financial and emotional nightmare.

By now you know I'm not saying you shouldn't have nice things. I believe God wants you to enjoy His blessings, and that includes buying some luxuries when you can afford them and when they make sense in your plan. Then, those things can be a blessing for you and your family, and you can have them because you want them, not because you want to impress other people. And I can tell you with 100 percent certainty that anything you buy with debt—no matter how much you enjoy it and no matter what it makes other people think of you—is *not* a blessing. "Well, Dave, how can you say that? Aren't you judging other people's purchases?" Yes, this is one time when I am! And I can back it up with Scripture. Proverbs 10:22 says, "The blessing of the LORD makes one rich, and He adds no sorrow with it." That last part is the key: "He adds no sorrow with it." Debt and payments are sorrowful. No one is excited or feels blessed because they *get* to make a ridiculous car payment every month. It's a burden, it is stealing their legacy, and it is absolutely *not* a blessing!

Even if you pay cash for these luxuries, they can still be ridiculously out of place if you go there too soon. For example, I don't think anyone should ever buy a brand-new car unless they have $1 million in net worth—even if they pay cash. The goal of your legacy journey is to make wise decisions over time, always taking care of the **NOW, THEN, US,** and **THEM,** and making sure that your giving, spending, and investing are proportional to your wealth. So if you're jumping the gun a little bit and spending too much money on stuff just to impress other people, stop it! You'll get there in time, but if you have a burning need to show other people your success, then you most likely have a discontentment problem.

Anxiety about What You Don't Have

"My name is Dave, and I like stuff."

I have to admit that I'm a recovering stuffaholic. As a kid and young adult, I was driven by the need to have and acquire more and more stuff. It was a huge problem that got me into big trouble when I was young. I don't struggle with that anymore, though, because it was burnt out of me the hard way—through bankruptcy court. Now that I use God's ways of handling money (and have for more than twenty-five years) and now that I understand my role as manager, freaking out about what I don't have isn't a big deal to me anymore.

When you struggle with discontentment, it's easy to get obsessed about what you don't have. This isn't about wealth or possessions. This is a spiritual problem where you're trying to fill a void in your life with some *thing*. The problem is, there's always *another* thing that you think will make you happy. And so you go through your whole life in an endless pursuit of stuff, always thinking that the *next* thing will be *the* thing that makes you happy. And when you buy it, that happiness lasts for about a second until you see something else you want. Then it starts all over again. I've been there. I've heard that voice in my head telling me that I *need* this or that. I've felt that pressure and anxiety about what I think is missing in my life. I can't think of many other things that will steal the joy of your success more than always being fixated on what you don't have.

If this is a problem for you, here's a tip: Cut yourself off from the source of the problem. For example, if you're a shopaholic, stop going to the mall. If you can't walk past a store without suddenly being overcome by the need to buy everything in the display window, then for heaven's sake just stay away from there! There's no such thing as window shopping when you struggle with a burning need for more stuff. Or if you're not ready to buy a new house, then don't go looking at houses. At best, you'll just come home frustrated and depressed. Or at worst, you'll make a stupid buying decision that could put your whole financial legacy in danger. Looking at more stuff, reading about more stuff, and fantasizing about more stuff isn't going to help you get past a sense of anxiety and panic over what you think is missing. It just feeds the beast, so stay away from it.

JEALOUSY AND ENVY

Probably the ugliest sign of discontentment is the one that's most common: jealousy and envy. I used to think these two words meant the same thing, but I was wrong. Now I know that there's a distinct difference between the two. Jealousy says, *I want what you have.* Envy, however, goes a step further. It says, *I want what you have, but I can't have what you have, and so I don't want you to have it either.* These two spirits are running wild in this culture today, and they're at the heart of a lot of the "wealth is evil" movement. If you go online for more than five minutes, I bet you'll read a rant about some evil rich guy wasting his money and how he should give it all to the poor.

I've already mentioned my friend Robert Morris, who pastors a huge church in Dallas. Robert is a great writer on the subject of generosity. It's a passion for him, and it's definitely a focus of his ministry. I've spent time at his church, and the whole congregation has an amazing spirit of generosity that obviously flows from the leadership down. Robert is one of those rare people who God has called to give everything away—twice. But again, this is rare. Even Robert will tell you that God doesn't call most people to give everything away. This was a specific calling on Robert's life at two specific times in his ministry. Please don't be confused about that. I'm just telling you that to give you a sense for Robert's heart for giving so you'll be able to understand what's coming next.

Robert's book *The Blessed Life* gives a fantastic picture of jealousy and envy at work:

> I once remember riding in the car with someone and passing by the large, beautiful home of a person who I knew to be a committed Christian and who had prospered by following biblical principles and giving generously.
>
> I pointed out the house to my driving companion and mentioned the owner's faith. His response was, "Well, he ought to sell that thing and give the money to the poor." Of course, the person making that comment was living in a house that was nicer than nine-tenths of the world's population could ever dream of owning. And guess what? He had no intention of selling his home and giving the money to [the poor].
>
> The ugly truth is that he didn't care about the poor.

He just resented the fact that someone had a nicer house than he did. A spirit of compassion didn't prompt the comment—a spirit of envy did.

This false spirituality manifests itself in several different but similar comments. See if any of these sound familiar: "How could anyone in good conscience drive a car that expensive?" "She sure could have helped a lot of people for what she spent on that coat." Or my personal favorite: "I could sure do a lot of good with the money they spent on that [insert name of luxury item here]." Remarks such as these are pure selfishness and jealousy dressed up as religious superiority—and it's ugly.[2]

The bottom line is that no amount of wealth can be called spiritual or unspiritual, and no one except you and God will truly know if you're being a wise or wasteful steward. And remember that you have a full-time job taking care of yourself, so don't bother trying to judge what anyone else should be doing with what God's given them to manage. He gives to each one according to His plan. Translation: Mind your own business!

IT'S ALL ABOUT RATIOS

One big reason why people criticize what others do with their wealth is that they are only looking at a dollar amount. The problem is, dollar amounts are relative. The amount doesn't change, but its relative worth changes big time based on the person's financial situation. For some families, giving $1,000 is a monumental, once-in-a-lifetime opportunity. For others, $1,000 is the amount they tithe to their church each week. What really matters here isn't the dollar amount, but the amount as a percentage of their income. For that, it all comes down to ratios.

Reality Check

Let's slow down for a minute to do a quick reality check. At this point in the Baby Steps, we'll assume that you have some wealth. I know that's not true for everyone, but for the sake of this discussion, I'm going to assume that you're out of debt, have a full emergency fund, are actively contributing 15 percent of your income into retirement, have your kids' college funding underway or taken care of, and you've paid off the house. Whew! Great job! If you're not there yet, don't worry about it. You'll get there. God's ways work, and if you keep plugging away, you'll be at this point a lot faster than you think. So with all that behind you, you're now into Baby Step 7 territory, which is building wealth and giving a bunch of it away.

What about the **NOW–THEN–US–THEM** model? Well, if you're at this point, it means that you've done a great job of taking care of the **NOW**, because everything is under control. The **THEN** is pretty much taken care of because you've been investing into retirement for a while and you've knocked out the mortgage. You're doing great with the **US**, because you're building wealth that will one day be passed generationally. And now it's time to kick the **THEM** stage into high gear. That's where you get serious about doing acts of mercy and evangelism for the kingdom with God's money. Sure, you've been tithing at every stage of the process, and once you got out of debt and got your emergency fund in place, you started doing some extra giving here and there. That's great!

But when you hit the **THEM** stage, your giving comes totally unglued. At this stage, you've lived like no one else, so now you get to give like no one else. Again, I know you may not be there yet. You may still be getting out of debt or building up your emergency fund. That's okay, but I need you to go here emotionally with me for this discussion. Imagine that you've just sent the last mortgage payment to the bank. You're sitting at the kitchen table looking at your checkbook, and you realize that you are completely free. The house is paid for, and you have $500,000 or $1 million in your retirement account. Then comes the question *What do I do now?* Let's talk about that.

Cups, Swimming Pools, and Thimbles

The size of your chalice—the amount needed to take care of your own household—is completely up to you and God. Never forget that. But that means you actually do need to figure out how big your cup should be. It's different for everyone; there is no magic number that fits every family or every income level. That's why no one—not even me—can look at your situation and tell you what that number should be. I will encourage you, though, to be balanced as you think through this. Like I said before, if you set it too high, you'll end up with a swimming pool, not a cup. That's where greed creeps in, and there won't be any overflow to give to others. And if you set it too low, you'll have a thimble. That means you'll be giving everything away and you won't have a realistic amount for your family to spend and enjoy.

Understanding Ratios

The best way I know to keep the size of your cup in balance is to use budget ratios. A ratio shows us a dollar amount based on a percentage of income, and I'm going to show you how to apply ratios to the overflow from your cup. You see, a ratio looks at the whole picture. Saying, "I'm going to give X percent of my overflow" is a lot different than saying, "I think I should give X dollars away." The dollar amounts are relative, remember? Setting specific dollar amounts for your giving breaks down over time. At some point in your wealth building, that dollar amount may be way too low, so your cup starts to look like a swimming pool. Or you might set it too high early on, and you'd be feeding your family out of a thimble. Ratios keep things in balance, and they keep you from going out of bounds.

There are a few things that we should always be doing with our money, regardless of our level of wealth. One of those things, of course, is giving. When we understand that God is the Owner, we remember that He's called us to be generous, joyful givers. If we're managing things well for the Owner, then we are definitely setting aside a portion of our income for giving—and at this stage, this is well beyond the tithe. If you're a Christian, giving a tithe to your church should be part of your budget no matter what Baby Step you're on. But when you're at Baby Step 6 or 7, you can (and should) kick it up a notch—or two or three.

The second thing you should do with the overflow is invest in the future. The Bible says, "In the house of the wise are stores of choice food and oil" (Proverbs 21:20 NIV). That means wise people save and invest money. At this stage, you're still investing into retirement funds, but you're also actively investing for wealth building. That creates more wealth to pass down generationally (Proverbs 13:22) and more wealth to give to others. In a sense, you can think of your wealth building as a way to grow the golden goose. The bigger the goose, the bigger the golden eggs you (and future generations) can generously give to others.

The third and final thing you should do with the overflow is enjoy a reasonable lifestyle based on your level of wealth. It's perfectly biblical (therefore right) to not only take care of your family, but also to actively enjoy a portion of what God's given you to manage. One of the biggest blessings that comes from using ratios is that it helps you maintain balance while keeping your heart in the right place. Luke's gospel says, "For where your treasure is, there your heart will be also" (Luke 12:34). I've heard so many people get that verse backward. People seem to think it's saying that you put your money where your heart is. Read it again: "For where your treasure is, there your heart will be also." To me, that's saying *our hearts follow our treasure*, not the other way around. You may not be a selfish, greedy jerk at the start, but if all you do is spend money on "me, me, me," then your heart will follow your dollars. Guess what that makes you over time? A selfish, greedy jerk. Planning out your legacy journey using ratios protects you from this because it sets guardrails on your spending. It's fine to spend money on yourself as your wealth grows; ratios simply help make sure you're not spending *all* of it on Jet Skis and Jacuzzis.

Planning Ratios

The goal is to look at the overflow and set ratios for each of those three areas. You'll decide what percentage to give, what percentage to invest, and what percentage to use on lifestyle. The first thing you have to do, though, is decide what size cup you need to take care of your family. If you are at Baby Step 7, you'll set your zero-based budget at whatever income level you choose. That will serve as the "Income" blank on your monthly budget, as though that were all you brought home. We're going to put ratios in place for anything over that amount, so be sure it isn't so high that there's no overflow and isn't so low that you and your family can't enjoy the blessings God's given you. You have to find the balance, which definitely means you need to talk to the Owner. Pray about it, and ask God to show you what income is appropriate for your family. Ask Him to bless this exercise too because this is your commitment to be a good manager of His resources.

Let me give you some examples, but keep in mind that these are just examples. Nowhere in this book will I tell you how big your cup should be or what percentages you should set for your ratios. Maybe you're on Baby Step 7 and you have an annual income of $80,000. You could go through this exercise and decide that your family could live well on $50,000, so you'd apply ratios to the remaining $30,000. Or maybe you're a doctor and you make $250,000 a year. You could pray about it and, together with your spouse, decide that your family would live well on $150,000, meaning you'd apply ratios to the remaining $100,000. See how this works? First you set the baseline, then you apply ratios to anything over that amount.

Before we start looking at how the math works on this, let me go ahead and give you a word of warning. I've said a dozen times now that only you and God can decide the size of your cup and assign ratios. Nevertheless, even after you spend time in prayer and feel good about the decisions you make, you should expect criticism. People will always think you should have done more, given more, and kept less. They'll question your spirituality if (and when) your numbers don't measure up to *their* standard of what is holy. This is honestly one of the hardest things about winning with money. Having people who have no idea what it's like to bear this responsibility question what you're doing with God's money is frustrating and heartbreaking, but you can't bend to their pressure. God's given you this money to manage, not them. Let them worry about what He's given them; you're responsible to the Owner, not the critics.

Ratios in Action

Okay, let's flesh out how all this works. I'm going to give you an example with real numbers to work with, but remember that this is just an *example*. The ratios and percentages we'll use are what worked for one family that I counseled years ago. I'm not saying this is what you should do yourself. That's between you and God. Also, the income we're going to work with is astronomical. I get that. I chose it on purpose because I want you to see that this system works no matter what your income is. But this is definitely not the average American income, so don't write me any crazy letters telling me my example is too high!

Over the years, I've had the opportunity to work with a lot of wealthy and famous people. I'm going to use one of those families for this example, but obviously I won't use the guy's name. I'll just tell you that it was an NFL player at the top of his game, and he had an income of around $10 million a year. That's a lot. That kind of salary may seem like a jackpot to most people, but for this family, it was a huge responsibility. He and his wife love Jesus; I prayed with him several times, and it was powerful. He has an amazing spiritual walk, and he is extremely concerned with managing God's money wisely.

Are you getting that this is a good man who took his responsibility as a manager seriously? Good.

The first time we talked, he said something like, "Dave, I don't know what to do with all this money. All my buddies just spend everything. They give it all to their family members who think they won the lottery. They're supporting friends who are engaged in toxic behaviors. They lose half of it in bad business deals because they didn't think things through. It just slips right through their fingers. But I feel a huge responsibility to manage this money for God, and I don't know what I'm supposed to do. Can you help?"

Isn't it weird to hear a guy making that much money be so insecure? The truth is, most of them are like that. All that money comes with a huge burden, and people don't often talk about managing wealth at a high level like we are in this book. That's why it scares so many people, and that's why we need to figure these things out.

I walked this couple through the same things we've talked about in this chapter. I told them about setting a baseline income and about ratios for extra giving, investing, and lifestyle. Their first obstacle was setting a reasonable income. They talked about it for a few minutes, and then he said, "Dave, we've talked about it, and I think we could live really well on $100,000 a year." Now this guy was making $10 million, and he said he wanted to live on $100,000. It was all I could do to not start laughing.

I said something like, "Nuh uh. Listen, you're doing really, really well. You've worked hard at your craft. God has blessed you tremendously. I think God would smile if you spent some of that money on yourself and your family. He's your Father, and He's excited that you're doing well. Let's try $400,000, okay? You've got $10 million; you're not really going to miss $400,000. Besides, you can always adjust things later if this isn't the right fit." He and his wife went home and prayed about it, and the next week we set his monthly budget income based on an annual income of $400,000. Then we had to run ratios on everything he made over that $400,000 mark.

The first thing we factored in was the tithe. They were already tithing on the $400,000 they set for their baseline income, so of course they were going to tithe on anything above that too. So that's 10 percent. The second thing to factor in was taxes. The government is definitely going to take their share of your wealth, so the couple figured on about 40 percent of their overflow going to taxes. That meant between tithe and taxes, they had 50 percent of their overflow left. For that, we applied ratios for extra giving, investing, and lifestyle.

The couple agreed that 10 percent felt like a good number for extra giving, so that's what they used. Again, this is above the tithe. By the way, for this guy, 10 percent is $1 million. That means he was tithing $1 million and then giving *another* $1 million away—every year. That's actually not too uncommon among people at this level, but that's not what you hear about from the media. This level of giving is so far beyond what most people can even fathom, so do you understand how completely crazy it sounds when people say things like, "He should give more"? Come on, people.

Next, this couple settled on 35 percent for extra investing for wealth building. Keep in mind that we're not talking about wealth building just for the sake of growing a big pile of money. The investments are building wealth for kingdom purposes, so in a sense, a big part of the extra investing is actually delayed giving. You're going to invest that money now so that you'll have more to give later. Kind of sounds like the Parable of the Talents, doesn't it?

If you followed the math in this example, you see that this left 5 percent for extra lifestyle spending. The couple hesitated on this one and almost threw that money back into extra giving, but the truth is, God wants you to enjoy your success. As long as you keep it in balance, there's absolutely nothing wrong with that. Remember, it's your heritage to enjoy what God's blessed you with (Ecclesiastes 5:19). So they put the remaining 5 percent toward extra lifestyle.

Let's review how this turned out in this particular over-the-top, but real-life example. Remember, they were making $10 million a year and had set $400,000 aside as their baseline income. Everything over that was considered overflow for ratios. In this example, that means this couple applied ratios to $9,600,000 of overflow. Based on what they decided, these were their actual numbers:

- Tithe for Overflow Ratio: 10% = $960,000
- Taxes for Overflow Ratio: 40% = $3,840,000
- Extra Giving for Overflow Ratio: 10% = $960,000
- Investing for Overflow Ratio: 35% = $3,360,000
- Extra Lifestyle for Overflow Ratio: 5% = $480,000
- Overflow Ratio Total: 100% = $9,600,000

Interesting to note that their overall plan (baseline income plus overflow) had 40% going to taxes, 10% to tithe, 9.6% to extra giving, and their spending on themselves was only 6.8% of their income. Remember, you apply whatever ratios or percentages you would like to your overflow above your baseline budget. If you're a Christian and you're deciding on your ratios, it is easy to start by assuming 50 percent of your extra will go to tithe and taxes. That leaves you 50 percent of your extra income for investing, giving, and lifestyle.

This exercise was a huge blessing for this family, and it has enabled them to not only grow their own wealth over the years but to also give generously, enjoy their success, and ensure that their wealth never leads them off the proverbial cliff emotionally or spiritually. It's done the same thing for my family, and I think it'll do the same for yours. And because it's based on a percentage of income, not on fixed dollar amounts, this works whether your overflow is $10,000 or $10 million.

A JOURNEY, NOT A DESTINATION

The apostle Paul wrote, "I have learned to be content whatever the circumstances. I know what it is to be in need, and I know what it is to have plenty. I have learned the secret of being content in any and every situation, whether well fed or hungry, whether living in plenty or in want" (Philippians 4:11–12 NIV). I love that last part: "whether well fed or hungry, whether living in plenty or in want." By the way, Paul wrote that while he was sitting in prison! Even in prison, Paul's contentment wasn't based on his circumstances. He knew that God is not necessarily concerned with shaping your circumstances; He's concerned with shaping your character. And God does that throughout the journey, in the good times and the bad, when you're doing well financially and when you're flat broke.

The world is addicted to "bigger and better," so the idea of actually slowing down and enjoying what you have before moving on to the next big thing is kind of a joke these days. But without contentment, your whole life will just be jumping from one thing to another, always hoping that the *next* thing will be the thing that will make you happy. That's just not going to happen. Remember: Contentment isn't a destination; it's not a place you get to. It's a manner of traveling. It's an attitude that influences everything you do with money. If you leave it out of your plan, you'll never feel like you have "enough" of anything. And trust me, that's no way to live.

CHAPTER FIVE

Your Work Matters

D id you ever imagine you'd have all this?"
The reporter's question hung in the air for several seconds. I've been interviewed for different things literally thousands of times over the years. Most of these people ask the same set of questions, so I can usually breeze through the answers kind of on autopilot. But this time there was something about that question that hit me funny. She was doing a story on the twentieth anniversary of our radio show, and I have to admit, I was feeling a bit nostalgic. I'd been thinking about all the ups and downs I'd experienced since God started me on this professional journey, and my head was full of memories. So when she asked me that question, for the first time in a long time, I was stuck. It took me a few seconds to get my thoughts together enough to give her a good answer.

I thought about my prayer journal from 1993. Back then, "all this" consisted of a brand-new local radio show heard only in Nashville and a little blue self-published book called

Financial Peace that had sold a few thousand copies. I was fresh out of bankruptcy, and I was fighting and clawing to make a living as I sketched out my dream career. I had a strong sense that God was calling me into something beyond real estate, which is what I'd been doing before, but I didn't know much about publishing or radio back then. I was making it up as I went along.

If you were to look in my actual prayer journal from 1993, you'd find a page where I listed some initial goals. The second goal on that list says, "high-touch support group concept; combination seminar and counseling." From those few words, I started teaching a twenty-six-week-long class called *Life After Debt*. I taught it live a few nights a week in my community. The first night I taught it, we set up 135 chairs. Only four people showed up. Today, more than twenty years later, that class is now *Financial Peace University*. It's taught on video in basically every city in the country, and millions of families have been through it.

A couple of years later, I had another written goal: Sell 50,000 copies of *Financial Peace*. At that point, I had only sold 7,000 copies, and most of those were sold out of the back of my car. Selling 50,000 in a year was a huge goal—and I didn't hit it. But over time, I ended up selling 50,000, and then 100,000, and today, *Financial Peace* has sold more than 2.5 million copies. That same year, I set a goal for our radio show. We were heard in only one city back then, and we started thinking about syndicating. I wrote a goal to be in twenty-five cities within a year. We didn't come close. A couple of years later, we had only gotten up to twelve cities. But today, we're up to more than five hundred stations with more than 8 million listeners and, as of this writing, we're the number three talk radio show in the country and the largest privately owned syndicated show.

So when that reporter asked, "Did you ever imagine you'd have all this?" my head was swimming with all this history. I replied, "Well . . . yes and no." See, I knew that there was a huge need in the country. I knew that people were hurting in the area of personal finance and that someone needed to stand in that gap to serve them and help them out of their mess. But at the same time, I never in a million years expected to be the guy God would use to do that on this scale. I'm just a boy from Antioch, Tennessee. I wasn't a great writer. I wasn't a trained speaker. I wasn't an old pro in radio. I wasn't wealthy. At the time, I was still paying off old debts and getting my own act together. I was only a couple of years past the mess that most of my clients and listeners were in. So when God opened my eyes to this huge need, my thought was, *Yeah, God, You're right. Somebody's got to do something to help these people. But until You find the right guy, I'll do what I can to help out.* That response probably made God laugh. I can picture Him reaching down, tapping me on the shoulder, and saying, "Nuh uh. I'm going to use *you*. People will see that if I can use a broke, broken, inexperienced hothead like you to do this, then it really is from Me!"

When we started out, I had no idea how hard this journey would be. I didn't realize how many hours, years, or air miles it would take. I didn't know how difficult it would be to watch my team grow from one to five to fifty to five hundred. And through it all, I still never got over the fact that God used me to do this work. That is the most humbling part. I remember early on, some older, wiser man told me, "Dave, success is a journey, not a destination." I had no idea what he meant. Now that I've been doing this for a while and I'm reaching old-man status myself, I think I finally get it. There has never been a single point in my career where I became "successful." God's been writing success in and out of my story the whole time.

Looking back, the whole journey has been satisfying to my soul, but I've never been confused about *whose* work it is. This was all God's work, and for some reason, He chose me to do it. That's been one of the biggest blessings of my life. The truth is, though, He does this for all of us. Jeremiah 29:11 says, "'For I know the plans I have for you,' declares the LORD, 'plans to prosper you and not to harm you, plans to give you hope and a future'" (NIV). I believe that God has a plan for each and every one of us, and that plan includes a job, a career, a calling to do a specific work while we're on this earth—whether it's a nine-to-five job, a dream that starts in your basement, or being a stay-at-home parent. That means our work matters to God, and what we do with our days has a huge impact on the legacy we leave behind.

WORK MATTERS

As we talk about work, I want to start by telling you what this chapter is *not*. I'm not here to give you a detailed, foolproof plan for finding the perfect job. We're not going to talk about what to wear to a job interview, how to figure out what you want to do with your life, or how to target and win over potential employers. If that's what you're looking for, I recommend you check out *48 Days to the Work You Love* by my friend Dan Miller. If you're looking for a more philosophical discussion about how to find the perfect job, you can read *Start* by Jon Acuff. You'll find a helpful summary of the *Start* concepts in the appendix of this book.

But as far as this chapter goes, I don't want this to be a *how-to* guide at all. Instead, I want it to be a *why-to* chapter. Why does work matter to God? Why should the right kind of work matter to us? How does the work we do impact the legacy we leave? Those are huge questions, and we're not going to answer them fully. However, as you work on your legacy journey, these are all things you need to carefully examine.

Nine Years of Your Life

Most people would consider the average American's working lifetime to be age twenty-five to age sixty-five. Of course, plenty of people start earlier than that, and plenty of people work well into their seventies, eighties, and even nineties. But for the sake of simple math, let's say that your working lifetime is right around forty years. If you work the average workday of eight hours and take three weeks off per year for vacation and personal time, that means you'll spend roughly 78,400 hours—almost nine years of your life—at work. That's nine years' worth of time you're not with your family, you're not at church, you're not doing mission work, and you're not doing any of the "important" things we think we're supposed to be doing with our lives. I meet so many people who struggle with this. They say things like, "Dave, I just feel so guilty. I feel like God's put me on earth to do something important, but I can't do it from my cubicle. What do I do?" I'll ask if they hate their job, and often they'll say, "Oh no! I love my job! We provide a valuable service that helps a lot of people, and we do it better than anyone else. I just wish I could spend more time doing what God wants me to do."

Why is it that we sometimes think God only blesses the work we do *outside* the office? If God's put us in a system where we'll spend forty years of our lives working, doesn't it make sense that *that work* matters to God too? We get in the habit of compartmentalizing our lives, thinking that we have to be one way at church, one way at home, and yet another way at work. Where I come from, we call that hypocrisy. I feel pretty strongly that God's called me to be *me*, and that doesn't change based on where I am or what I'm doing. If I matter to God, and if God's given me something to do for forty hours a week, then that must mean my work matters to Him.

Work Is Important to God

Work is a major theme all throughout the Bible. It seems like you can't make it through a single chapter in Proverbs without reading about the rewards of diligence and the dangers of laziness. Proverbs 13:4 says, "The soul of a lazy man desires, and has nothing; but the soul of the diligent shall be made rich." Proverbs 10:4 says, "He who has a slack hand becomes poor, but the hand of the diligent makes rich." Probably my favorite of these is Proverbs 21:5: "The plans of the diligent lead surely to plenty, but those of everyone who is hasty, surely to poverty." Tracking this theme through Proverbs is fascinating. If you've never read the whole book, I'd encourage you to read one chapter of Proverbs a day for a month (it's easy since there are thirty-one chapters). As you read, make a note in your Bible every time you see a reference to work or laziness. That exercise could be a game changer for you.

Isn't it interesting that over and over again, Scripture says the result of laziness is poverty, but the result of hard work (diligence) is wealth? That's why I've said for years that your greatest wealth-building tool is your income. Think about that: What does your income represent? Getting a paycheck regularly is the reward for diligence. If you keep showing up at work, they keep paying you. Big shock, I know. But too many people get distracted with get-rich-quick gimmicks or high-risk investing because they want to get rich overnight. Instead of building wealth one day at a time over the course of many years, they want a shortcut. They act like there's a big, mysterious secret to becoming very wealthy, and if they sit on the sofa and think about it long enough, they'll figure it out. That's just not going to happen, but careful, diligent management of your income over a long period of time allows practically anyone to become a millionaire.

When you're relaxing in a rocking chair in twenty or forty years, you can never forget Who gave you the work that enabled you to build wealth. In Chapter 4, we saw how our ability to work, the days to work, the reward of work, and the enjoyment of that reward all come from God (Ecclesiastes 5:18–19). Everything about our work is His. If you ever get confused about that, remember what the Bible says in Deuteronomy:

> You may say to yourself, "My power and the strength of my hands have produced this wealth for me." But remember the LORD your God, for it is he who gives you the ability to produce wealth, and so confirms his covenant, which he swore to your ancestors, as it is today. (8:17–18 NIV)

If God gives us the ability to produce wealth through hard work, then we have to treat that like a special gift from our Father. He could make it rain gold coins if He wanted to, but instead, He gave us work. That's a biblical truth that goes all the way back to Adam in the Garden of Eden.

Warning against Idleness

As I read the New Testament, I see that the apostle Paul didn't have much patience for idle hands. The church at Thessalonica was a particular sore spot in this area. Certain members of that church had become so convinced that Jesus was returning any day that they stopped working. They thought, *Why should I go to work today if Jesus is coming back tomorrow?* Instead, they sat around not doing anything except eating other families' food and becoming gossipy busybodies! Paul hit this bunch pretty hard in 2 Thessalonians 3:6–12:

> In the name of the Lord Jesus Christ, we command you, brothers and sisters, to keep away from every believer who is idle and disruptive and does not live according to the teaching you received from us. For you yourselves know how you ought to follow our example. We were not idle when we were with you, nor did we eat anyone's food without paying for it. On the contrary, we worked night and day, laboring and toiling so that we would not be a burden to any of you. We did this, not because we do not have the right to such help, but in order to offer ourselves as a model for you to imitate. For even when we were with you, we gave you this rule: "The one who is unwilling to work shall not eat." We

hear that some among you are idle and disruptive. They are not busy; they are busybodies. Such people we command and urge in the Lord Jesus Christ to settle down and earn the food they eat. (NIV)

The model Paul says we should imitate is one of hard work, where we strive to take care of our own needs and not become a burden to others. That doesn't mean there won't be times when we need help; we've all been in a bad spot from time to time when the kindness of other people or the church was the only thing that got us through the storm.

What Paul is talking about here is an overriding attitude of laziness and idleness, acting as though our needs were someone else's responsibility. That's simply not a biblical position. When we discussed the meaning of **NOW** in the **NOW–THEN–US–THEM** framework, we saw that our first duty is to do what it takes to provide for our families: "If anyone does not provide for his own, and especially for those of his household, he has denied the faith and is worse than an unbeliever" (1 Timothy 5:8). Our work matters to God, if for no other reason than it is the means by which we take care of our families—and that's our top financial priority.

Work Is Creative

My friend Rabbi Lapin, who I've already mentioned a couple of times, once told me, "Man is most in God's image when he is creating things." I love that line because I'm a creative guy. I love to come up with new ways to communicate information, and I surround myself with people who are better at it than I am. That's why my company is involved in so many different forms of media, from web to video to books to live events. Our company's mission statement sums it all up: "We provide biblically based, common-sense education and empowerment that give HOPE to everyone in every walk of life." Everything we do is focused on that one thing, and we fire all our creative cannons at making that happen.

For example, I remember the first time I sat down with some of my team members to discuss the topics that would ultimately become *The Legacy Journey* class, which preceded this book. We knew people wanted a follow-up to our *Financial Peace University* class, but we never make a new product just because we need something new to sell. Everything we do has to have a purpose, so some of us sat around my conference table one night and talked about whether or not God was calling us to create a new high-level discussion on wealth, contentment, and extreme generosity. As we talked that night, every single one of us lit up as we worked through new ideas and concepts. We felt an undeniable energy in the conversation, and there wasn't a person in the room who didn't think God was calling us to do something new. That started a months-long process of planning, meeting, writing, editing, and designing. One team was focused on capturing just the right message. Another team was responsible for the video shoot. Another team went to work on all the design elements. Another team planned the live event where we'd shoot the video. And I got to sit in and over all of it, watching God knit this new thing together. It was a blast! Those are always some of the most exciting, most rewarding days I ever have because that's when we're in our zone, creating brand-new things out of nothing. The times I've done that the best are the times in my life when I have felt closest to God, when it seems like we're riding the wave of the Holy Spirit. It's amazing!

So when you are creating, dreaming something, then helping it to be born, you are truly acting like you were made in God's image. Find some things to do that give you that child-like excitement periodically in your career. Your work, your life, everything about you—it all matters to God.

Finding Purpose in Activity

In today's culture, so many people are wandering around in what I call *professional limbo*. They spend most of the day sitting around doing nothing. If you ask them if they are looking for a job, they'll say they want to figure out their purpose first. It's as though the very idea of taking an entry-level position at a good company is incomprehensible. Sure, they'll stay on government unemployment for two years, but filing papers, cleaning houses, or waiting tables is somehow beneath them. It doesn't make sense. Whether you're just out of school or newly out of work, get out there and do something! There are always pizzas to be delivered, houses to be cleaned, and lawns to be cut. I have a friend who says, "Residential landscaping is a gold mine. Rich people are scared of leaves!" One leaf blower may be all it takes to feed your family for months!

The key is activity. If your family is struggling or even if you're trying to launch your career from scratch, sitting around thinking about your "purpose" can be a form of procrastination. You'll end up like Cousin Eddie in *Christmas Vacation*, who was out of work for seven years because he was "holding out for a management position." Let me tell you what you *should* be managing: Your life. Your family. Your legacy. You can't find your purpose on your couch, unless your purpose is spare change. Get out there and move some things around, and your purpose will find you. It's called the Butterfly Effect and it means: A little bit of activity today can lead to enormous results later. You never know what the final result of any action will be. Doing something—anything—today may be the thing that leads you to the thing that leads you to the thing that leads you to the *perfect* thing for you. It's not going to be a clear, easy-to-follow journey, and you're not going to step from the starting line immediately to the finish line. There's a whole race to be run between those points, so don't worry if you can't see the finish line yet. You're not supposed to. You can't control the finish line. As Jon Acuff says, "The only line you control is the starting line." You've got to get started. There are no results without activity.

I'll give you one warning, though. Some people take their professional activity way too far—to unhealthy extremes. Now, I'm a huge fan of work. I *love* to work and to work hard. I surround myself with people who do the same. Everyone at our office is passionate about what they do. Most of them would probably stay there all night half the week if we let them. But here's the thing: We don't let them. We work hard, but at 5:30 every evening, it's time to shut down the computers and leave. We take the passion and enthusiasm home with us and pour it into our families. We work hard, sure, but we also play hard. We don't get confused about what's really important in our lives.

Sometimes we'll bring a new web programmer or publishing person on board who came from a business where eighty-hour workweeks were the norm. They can have a hard time adjusting to the way we do things, and so we have to help them by kicking them out the door at 5:30 p.m. The work we do and the work you do is important, but it's not more important than our marriages and children. I often tell my team that I refuse to become a success with a trail of divorces and broken homes behind me. Don't let that happen to your family either. Be passionate at work, but be more passionate at home.

SUCCESS STARTS IN YOUR HEART

I talk to dozens of people about their money every day on my radio show. A lot of these men and women are calling because they want to get out of debt and they want to know how to do it. I can always tell which ones are serious and which aren't. There's something in their voices that communicates passion and conviction when they're really excited about getting out of debt. But if they're just playing around with the idea, if they're simply curious about it, then their voices are flat. If I don't hear any passion behind what they're saying, I know they aren't ready to cut up the credit cards and dump their debt for good. That's because getting out of debt isn't about solving a math problem; it's about changing your life—and that requires a change of heart. Proverbs says, "Above all else, guard your heart, for everything you do flows from it" (4:23 NIV). That means everything of value in my life—from getting out of debt to my career to my relationships to my wealth building—starts in my heart.

The Strangest Secret
I'm a big fan of goal setting and positive thinking. I guess I can thank my parents for that. Mom and Dad were real estate

agents, and they were good at it. They knew how to sell, and any good salesperson knows that a big part of being successful in sales is keeping a steady stream of positive thoughts running through your head. They taught me early on that if I want to win, I have to imagine myself winning. If I want to build wealth, I have to imagine myself building wealth. If I want a good marriage . . . If I want to raise great kids . . . If I want to grow in my faith . . . It all starts in the mind and heart, "for everything you do flows from it" (Proverbs 4:23 NIV).

Because of that attitude, my parents were always listening to sales-training and personal-development audiotapes every time they got in the car. That means little Dave Ramsey, riding in the backseat during long road trips, got a master's degree in positive thinking by age ten. Some of my favorite memories are of my family driving to a vacation spot while listening to the greats like Zig Ziglar, Charlie "Tremendous" Jones, and, of course, Earl Nightingale.

Nightingale's powerful message *The Strangest Secret* got stuck in my brain from an early age. I remember hanging on every word of that audio presentation while sitting in the back of my parents' car. It's a message I've probably come back to a hundred times in the forty-five years since. What is "the strangest secret"? It's the simplest thing in the world: We become what we think about. Our thoughts are directly tied to our results. It sounds almost biblical, doesn't it? Nightingale explains:

> I want to tell you about a situation that parallels the human mind. Suppose a farmer has some land. And it is good fertile land. Now, the land gives the farmer a choice. He may plant in that land whatever he chooses.

The land doesn't care. It's up to the farmer to make the decision.

. . . Now let's say that the farmer has two seeds in his hand—one is a seed of corn, the other is nightshade, a deadly poison. He digs two little holes in the earth and he plants both seeds, one corn, the other nightshade. He covers up the holes, waters, and takes care of the land. And what will happen?

Invariably, the land will return what's planted. As it's written in the Bible, "As ye sow, so shall ye reap." Now remember, the land doesn't care. It will return poison in just as wonderful abundance as it will corn. So up come the two plants: one corn, one poison.

The human mind is far more fertile, far more incredible and mysterious than the land, but it works the same way. It doesn't care what we plant—success or failure, a concrete, worthwhile goal or confusion, misunderstanding, fear, anxiety, and so on. But what we plant must return to us.

The human mind is the last great, unexplored continent on earth. It contains riches beyond our wildest dreams. It will return anything we want to plant.[1]

But the key is, you have to plant something. You have to put something in your mind and work toward it. That's called a goal, and more than anything else in the world, setting and striving toward goals will determine whether or not you are a success in life. Earl Nightingale defined success as "the progressive realization of a worthy ideal," or goal. Notice that he didn't say it's the *accomplishment* of a goal; it's the progressive realization—the act of working toward the goal. So when are you a success? You're a success when you get off the couch, set a good goal, and get to work! The minute you take that first step toward a goal, you become successful. Success isn't really about *reaching* the goal—although it's best if you do; it's about setting your mind on something and doing what it takes to make that goal a reality. That's when you change your life.

My friend Zig Ziglar once said, "By altering our attitudes, we can alter our lives." That's true. It starts in our hearts and minds. Author Robin Sharma took that idea a step further: "Everything is created twice: first in the mind, and then in reality."[2] Think about that. When an artist gets ready to paint a picture, she has to create it in her mind before the brush ever hits the canvas. Before a builder builds a house, someone has to dream up what that house will look like. Before you write a book, you have to have an idea of what you want to say. You get the idea. The bottom line is that you can't do a single thing in your job, family, or finances that doesn't start in your mind. The human mind is one of the most powerful God-given forces in all of Creation, and we each get the opportunity to steer and direct that force every day of our lives! So here's an idea: Take control of what's in your mind!

How many times did Jesus talk about the power of faith, of simply *believing*? He said, "According to your faith let it be done to you" (Matthew 9:29). "As you have believed, so let it be done for you" (Matthew 8:13). "Ask, and it will be given to you; seek, and you will find; knock, and it will be opened to you" (Matthew 7:7). "If you have faith and do not doubt, . . . you [can] say to this mountain, 'Be removed and be cast into the sea,' [and] it will be done" (Matthew 21:21). Are you seeing a theme here? Belief matters. Setting your mind on something and believing it's not only *possible* but *probable* is the key to success. I want to be clear here, though. I'm not talking about simply dreaming. Dreaming doesn't get you anywhere if you don't take the next step and tie it to a goal. We're striving for a progressive realization of a goal, not the endless repetition of a dream. Dreams are a great start, but a dream that's ready to go to work becomes a goal.

Finding the Sweet Spot

A goal takes what starts in your mind and turns it into reality. It puts action to the creative force we've talked about. I told you that when we first started syndicating our radio show, I wrote a goal to go from one to twenty-five cities within a year. Once that idea became a goal, I had to get to work. It wasn't going to happen accidentally. Now, like I said, we didn't hit that goal for several years, but it gave us a target. By writing it down, my team and I were able to start working toward that goal. Whether we hit it within the time frame we set or not, according to Earl Nightingale, we were *already* successful just because we were moving toward a worthy goal.

If you look at my early goals for the radio show, the *Financial Peace* book, and our *Financial Peace University* class, one thing really stands out: The goals were just out of reach. We didn't hit any of them in the time frame we set. Does that mean we failed? No way! Remember, you're a success when you start working toward a goal. We had a target, and we got to work. It took several years to hit those first few goals, but we got there. And by the time we reached them, we were emotionally mature enough to handle the responsibility that went along with that level of success. God has a way of preparing you for the success that comes with reaching your goals while you're in the process of working toward them. That might be why some people seem to win overnight while it takes others a while to get there. Maybe God's working some things out in those people's lives along the journey. I know He did with me.

When you set goals for your life, you need to set them slightly out of your reach. Picture yourself reaching as far as you can, and then set your goal a few inches past that, where your fingertips can barely touch it. Jim Collins and Jerry Porras, authors of *Built to Last*, call that a BHAG: a Big Hairy Audacious Goal. You know what that does? It leaves room for the power of God. There's a delicate balance between setting realistic, achievable goals and leaving room for the power of God to work. You don't want to set easy goals that you could almost stumble into just to make sure you reach them. And you also don't want to set goals that are so crazy and impossible that you'll never be motivated to work toward them. You want to leave room for the power of God, but that doesn't mean you can set a completely unrealistic goal and then simply sit back and wait for God to make it happen. That's not a goal; that's a dream. Remember, goals put you to *work*!

Have you ever held some food or a chew toy up in the air to encourage a dog to jump? If you hold it too high, the dog will know there's no way he can reach it, so he won't even try. If you hold it too low, the dog will get the prize once or twice and then get bored. But there's a sweet spot, where if you hold the toy in just the right spot—high enough to make it a challenge but low enough to make it seem achievable—that will keep the dog jumping all day. That's where you want to set your goals.

The Wheel of Life

I've studied the practice of goal setting for a long time, and one, distinct paradigm continues to rise to the surface. Zig Ziglar called it the Wheel of Life. Picture a big wheel with spokes dividing the wheel into seven segments. The wheel is your life, and the seven sections are the key parts that make up your life. These are all specific areas that we have to be intentional about in our goal setting. The seven areas are Career, Intellectual, Financial, Social, Physical, Spiritual, and Family.

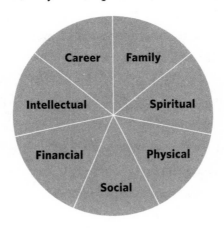

For an overall healthy life, you need to set goals in each of these seven areas. As you look at the list, you'll no doubt see a couple that come naturally to you. For example, the career and financial spokes have always come easy for me. I've always been able to make money. I used to have trouble *keeping* it, but I was always able to *make* it! Career-wise, I come up with a dozen new business ideas every day before breakfast. Most of them stink, but a few of them turn out to be pretty good. I'm just wired that way, so setting goals in those two areas is a breeze.

Social, on the other hand, is definitely my weakest area. I love people, and I love big crowds of people, but forced and concocted social events make me want to scream. The idea of standing over a plate of finger foods and going through the whole "What do you do?" exchange sends me running for the hills. I'm convinced that if I wasn't married, I wouldn't have any friends outside of work!

So every year, I set goals for myself in each of these seven areas. I don't give myself a pass on social just because I stink at it. In fact, I'm *more* intentional about my social goals because if I don't write them down and hold myself accountable to them, they'll never get done. The point here is that you want to keep growing in every area of life. You'll always have areas where you excel and some where you struggle, but you want the wheel to keep turning. Zig Ziglar used to say that if you ignore one area, your wheel gets a flat spot. That leads to a flat tire, which makes it harder to move forward in life. You'll waste a lot of time, effort, and energy trying to push a flat tire, so you have to make sure every part of the wheel gets your attention.

I want to give you one word of warning, though. There are some who say you should always strive for balance in your life. That is, you always have to maintain a certain tension between all of these different areas to make sure you're not focusing too much on one area to the exclusion of the others. They may call it a "work-life balance" or "balanced life." That's a trap. The truth is, there will never be a time in your life when everything is perfectly balanced. If you're trying to launch a new business, you're going to spend more time in the career area. If you're trying to lose weight or run a marathon, you're going to spend more time in the physical area. If you're up to your eyeballs in debt and set a goal to be debt-free, you're going to spend more time in the financial area. Trying to give equal time to every area and every goal will practically guarantee failure. I believe in a balanced life, but that's a big-picture view. My goal is to look back over my life over a long period of time and feel good about the whole thing, not about where I spent my time in any specific day, week, or month. You never want to ignore any area—especially your family—but trying to evenly divide twenty-four hours a day across all seven areas will drive you insane and leave you exhausted.

Five Guidelines for Good Goals

Many people I talk to are terrified of writing goals. They act as though they're carving these things into marble instead of writing them down on a legal pad. Then, if something goes wrong or they fall short, they end up with a cloud of guilt over their heads that keeps them from moving forward. If that's you, you need to relax. Goal setting isn't rocket science, and you get to control every part of the goal. It's like doing a budget: I don't care *what* you spend your money on; I just want you to write it down and spend your money on purpose. With the Wheel of Life, I don't really care what your goals are; I just want you to write them down and do them on purpose too! So take a breath, let go of any anxiety you feel, and write down a few *good* goals. You can do that by making sure your goals follow five guidelines:

1. Your goals must be specific.
2. Your goals must be measurable.
3. Your goals must have a time limit.
4. Your goals must be your own.
5. Your goals must be in writing.

The starting point for every goal is to make sure it's specific and measurable. "I want to lose weight" is not a goal; it's a wish. A goal has to be specific, and you have to know what winning looks like. So instead, you could say, "I want to lose thirty pounds." That gives you a definite target to aim for, and there will be no ambiguity about whether or not you reach it.

Next, your goals must have time limits. By what date do you want to lose thirty pounds? Sometime in the next decade? That won't work, because you'll never be motivated to get started. Instead, you could say, "I want to lose thirty pounds in three months." Now we're cooking. From there, you can break the goal down into bite-sized pieces. Thirty pounds in three months is ten pounds per month, or two-and-a-half pounds a week. At this point, specific, measurable, and timed are all working together to keep you on track.

But *why* do you want to lose thirty pounds? If it's because your spouse wants you to, it'll never happen. Your goals must be your own. You'll never stay motivated and make the sacrifices needed to win if you're chasing *someone else's* goals. But if it's a goal that you're passionate about, one that you've fully embraced and made your own, then you'll do whatever it takes to make it happen.

The last step is the one that most people overlook: Your goals must be in writing. Habakkuk 2:2 says, "Write the vision and make it plain." There is spiritual power in writing down your goals. Something happens in your heart when you take an idea out of your mind, carefully articulate it into a goal, and then write it down. Having it in writing keeps it in front of you. It holds you accountable. Again, you set your own goals, but once you write them down, you become accountable to that piece of paper. It's your measuring stick. That's what shows you if and how you're winning.

SUCCESS IS A PROGRESSION

I have a confession to make. I wasn't a great leader twenty-five years ago. I also didn't know much about being a great husband or father back then. I was terrible at managing my money, and I was heading into bankruptcy because of my own financial stupidity. I was an immature, baby Christian in those days too. By the grace of God, I'm better at all of those things now. It didn't happen overnight, but over the course of years and decades, by setting goals and striving to reach them, by working hard "as to the Lord" (Colossians 3:23), God grew me in every one of those areas and more.

The truth is, every successful person I know is a failure. They have a long line of failures behind them—goals they fell short on or mistakes that threatened to derail their plans. Some of them, like me, actually *did* have their plans derailed because they weren't on the paths God had set for them. God had to step in and do some course corrections. This has definitely been true in my life. I absolutely love what I get to do for a living, and it's truly my life's calling. However, if you were to ask that young, hotshot real-estate wiz in his twenties what he wanted to do with his life, he wouldn't have had a clue. He would have thought the next forty years would be an unending string of bigger and better house flips and investment properties. Spending decades helping people with their money wouldn't have even been an option. Fortunately for me,

God stepped in and set my life on the journey He mapped out for me. He'll do the same for you.

So let's review: Work creates wealth. Work done as a career is more satisfying and usually pays better. But the best possible scenario is to begin working (no couches) so that you can run into opportunity, then polish that opportunity into a career. Then if you continue to polish and pray, while finding your passions, setting goals, and directing your thoughts toward success, your career will fully blossom into a calling. When you work in your calling, you are creative, talented, passionate, and intentional as unto the Lord, which will likely cause you to build wealth over time from an ever-increasing income. This progression is quite the opposite of people who never change, never grow, never set goals, and then stagnate in the marketplace. These people don't have twenty years of experience; they have one year's experience repeated twenty times. See the difference?

If you are going to be intentional about your wealth building, estate planning, and legacy journey, then you must be intentional about developing your calling into a wonderfully fulfilling, productive, and prosperous part of your life and your spiritual walk.

We said at the beginning of this chapter that success is a journey, not a destination—and I believe God's got big plans for every one of us. Scripture says, "'For I know the plans I have for you,' declares the LORD, 'plans to prosper you and not to harm you, plans to give you hope and a future'" (Jeremiah 29:11 NIV). He's got the whole journey already mapped out! That doesn't mean we can just sit back and wait for Him to carry us every step of the way, though. We've got to get off the couch, throw a brick through the television, and get to work.

CHAPTER SIX

Safeguarding Your Legacy

I have a good friend whose father was a two-term governor of our state—the youngest governor in the state's history, in fact. So my buddy spent eight years as a little boy in the Governor's Mansion. That family spent their time and energy invested in politics. Their dinner table conversations were about public service. Just by sitting at the table, he learned everything his dad knew about how to govern wisely. Is it any wonder that my friend grew up to become a US congressman? I have another friend whose father was a master mechanic. Growing up, he and his dad talked shop all the time. They spent several hours a week lying under or leaning over cars, rebuilding engines, and talking about carburetors. My friend soaked it up like a sponge. Is it any wonder that my friend grew up to be a serious gearhead? In both of these cases, the sons received an inheritance—a legacy —of love, time, attention, and resources that shaped their futures. They weren't little robots with no choice in what they would do with their lives; they were boys whose dads had shared their passions with their sons, and that passion became a family tradition. It was woven into the environments they grew up in.

The cool thing is that you get to choose the environment your kids grow up in. You can set the tone, the conversation, the shared passions—all of it. Of course, as your kids develop their own personalities, they're going to have interests of their own, and they may not like what you like. Believe me, I've got three kids, and they're all totally different! But the one thing they have in common is that they all grew up under my roof, and they all shared the experience of what it meant to grow up as a Ramsey. My wife, Sharon, and I were intentional about what we did and what we talked about. We taught them about God's ways of handling money and how to live for other people. Now that they're all grown up, they have different personalities and interests, but their core values are tied directly to the inheritance Sharon and I passed on to them.

As I've talked to literally hundreds of millionaires—and even a few billionaires—over the years, I've noticed that practically every super-wealthy family of faith is intentional about preparing their children to shoulder the financial responsibility of generational wealth. All you see on TV are the drama queens and train-wreck stories, but in real life, godly wealthy people take this responsibility very, very seriously. That's because they love their children, and they want this generational wealth to be a blessing for them. Nobody wants to ruin their kids' lives! But that's exactly what wealth does if it's passed down to adult children who don't have the emotional and spiritual backbone to carry it. So just like political families talk about politics, wealthy families talk about wealth. It shapes the conversations around the dinner table.

But kids are just one part of the equation. If you really want to build a legacy that lasts, you have to be intentional about safeguarding that legacy against anyone and anything that could tear it apart. That's what we're going to cover in this chapter.

THE SAFEGUARD PARADIGM

As I've had the opportunity to talk to a lot of wealthy people (and people working to become wealthy), one of the most common questions I get is this: "Dave, as you and Sharon went broke and then rebuilt your wealth, how did you keep the new wealth from ruining your life, your marriage, and your kids?" That surprised me the first few times I heard it, but then I started to understand the heart of the question. How many times have we seen wealth poison a family? How many spoiled, crazy rich kids make headlines for running their lives off the rails? How many friendships have been destroyed because one guy got wealthy and his buddies were hurt or confused by it? We see it everywhere, and if we don't take steps to protect our relationships from it, it could happen to any of us. That's what I mean when I talk about "safeguards." We want to put guardrails in place to keep our wealth from running our lives and relationships into a ditch. This chapter is all about the **US** of the **NOW–THEN–US–THEM** framework. This is where we'll talk about protecting our closest relationships—the **US**—from the dangers of wealth.

Blessings or Curses?

Deuteronomy 30:19 says, "I call heaven and earth as witnesses today against you, that I have set before you life and death, blessing and cursing; therefore choose life, that both you and your descendants may live." Obviously, that passage is talking about the decision to obey the Lord, but I think we can see this as a financial principle as well. You see, as your wealth expands, so do your opportunities to choose either blessings or curses, life or death, for future generations.

The decisions you make at each step of your legacy journey dictate the type of legacy you'll leave. If you're intentional about protecting your marriage, teaching your kids about money, giving generously, managing your wealth using ratios, and maintaining healthy relationships, then you'll leave not only a powerful, enduring financial legacy, but also a legacy of love and respect that will last several generations. However, if you aren't serious about these things and you just try to wing it, your wealth will be a curse to future generations. Your financial success could be responsible for a broken marriage, spoiled-rotten kids, and a legacy of greed and destruction. No one wants to be remembered that way. So, in order to protect your future legacy, you have to safeguard your life today.

Four Areas through Three Lenses

We can safeguard our legacy by being vigilant in four key areas. If you're lazy in any one of these areas, you could put your entire legacy in jeopardy. The first area is your personal life—your legacy as an individual. This is crucial whether you are single or married, and whether you have kids or not. Who you are as an individual influences every other relationship in your life, so we have to be careful here. The second area is your marriage—your legacy as a couple. What are the traps that could endanger your marriage? The third area is your children—your legacy as a family. What are you doing to proactively protect your kids from the dangers of wealth? The fourth and last area is other relationships in your life—your legacy as a friend and extended family member. There are all kinds of problems that could pop up in any one of those relationships. So if you want your wealth to be a blessing instead of a curse, you have to make sure you're actively protecting each area.

How do we do that? I believe it comes down to viewing each of these four areas through three lenses: ownership (whose is it?), magnification (what does it do to each area?), and community (how does it affect those around me?). And I'll say up front that the Ramsey family is not perfect. We've done a lot of these things really well, but we've also done some of it poorly in the past. That's why we call this a legacy *journey*—we're not there yet. However, I think we've figured out some things along our journey as a family. We've gotten the bumps and bruises, and we've gotten a lot of them under the microscope of public scrutiny. If you host a national radio show telling people how they can build wealth, you better believe there are plenty of people out there watching and waiting for you to mess up. But so far, with God's help and by being intentional in these key areas, we haven't had any major problems.

That's the safeguard paradigm: four relationship areas through three lenses. We'll view our personal lives, marriages, kids, and other relationships through the lens of ownership, magnification, and community. It sounds like a lot, but it breaks down pretty simply. Stick with me!

PERSONAL LIFE: MY LEGACY AS AN INDIVIDUAL

In the previous chapter, we talked about Proverbs 4:23: "Above all else, guard your heart, for everything you do flows from it" (NIV). Think about that for a minute: "everything you do." That means your walk with Christ, your relationship with your spouse, how you interact with your children, the way you operate your business, how you manage your money, how you act around your friends . . . it all flows out of your heart. I learned a long time ago that if I wanted to serve the Lord, have quality relationships, and win with money, I had to take control of the guy in the mirror. He was the only thing holding me back. He was the only one who could ruin everything God wanted to do in and through me. As you work on safeguarding your legacy, the first and most important area you need to manage is yourself.

The Ownership Lens

"Hey, dummy. You don't own anything."

Sometimes that's the first thing I tell myself when I wake up in the morning. I've already told you that I'm a recovering stuffaholic. I like stuff. God's blessed my family, and we have some nice stuff, but I'm not confused about Who really owns it. Psalm 24:1 says, "The earth is the LORD's, and the fulness thereof" (KJV). It's His. It's *all* His. I'm a car guy, and love my car. But every time I get behind the wheel, I have to emotionally remind myself that God gave me that car, and if He tells me to give it away, I will. That's His right, because He's the owner. He could do the same with my house, my business, my money, or anything else because it's not mine. "The earth is the LORD's"—the whole thing.

But you know what's even scarier? That also means that *my family* belongs to the Lord. I love my wife and kids more than anything on earth, and as a loving husband and father, it's hard for me to put those lives and relationships in His hands. I'm a doer; I'm always doing something or working on something. Finding the spiritual discipline to sit back and trust the most precious thing in my life—my family—to God is probably the hardest thing for me to do when it comes to recognizing God's ownership. However, as I read the Scriptures, I don't see any exclusions to the "God owns it all" principle.

If you ever get confused about this, just look at Job. God blessed Job more than possibly anyone else on earth at the time, but then God took it all back—even Job's children. I can't even imagine that. And as Job is sitting there grieving, and as his friends are giving him bad advice, what does God say? "Who has a claim against me that I must pay? Everything under heaven belongs to me" (Job 41:11 NIV). God had to step in and remind Job that He owns *everything under heaven*. But that's good news! God's hands are big enough to hold it all; mine aren't. If I want what's best for my family (or my wealth or my legacy), then I'm going to entrust it to God's care. I'm grateful to be a steward of all these blessings, but I have to constantly remind myself to hold them all with an open hand.

Not owning, but managing, changes not only our view of things, but also our process of handling them. For some reason, we do a better job taking care of things we manage than things we own. Making decisions about giving, saving, spending, and managing money like you were in charge of someone else's money changes your decisions and behaviors. The big thing about releasing ownership is that, when you do, you don't feel puffed up or entitled. Releasing ownership brings a type of financial humility.

The Magnification Lens

When it comes to our legacy, the magnification principle boils down to this: More money makes you more of what you already are. Whatever you are—good or bad—is going to get bigger when you add wealth to the mix. If you're a jerk with nothing, you'll be a colossal jerk with money. If you have a little temper problem when you're broke, you'll be an out-of-control rageaholic with wealth. That's the downside. But the reverse is true too. If you're compassionate and generous with a little, then wealth will turn you into a world-changing philanthropist. If you do acts of mercy with no money, then more money will enable you to bless people beyond their (or your) imaginations—and they'll probably never even know it was you doing it, because wealthy givers tend to stay anonymous. They'd rather God get the credit because they're not confused about ownership.

I think this is a big part of what Scripture means when it talks about being a faithful steward. The Bible says "a person who is put in charge as a manager must be faithful" (1 Corinthians 4:2 NLT). Stewardship isn't only about what you *do* with God's resources; it's also about your attitude while doing it. We see over and over in Proverbs that wise people prosper and foolish people don't. Why? Is it just because wise people know how to save and invest? That's part of it, but maybe—just maybe—the simple fact that they are wise puts them in a position to win. It's magnification, remember? If you're wise with a little, you'll be a genius with a lot; if you're foolish with a little, you'll be an unstoppable idiot with a lot! Who you are, what you do, and what you believe matter.

The Community Lens

I've heard several leadership and relationship coaches say that everyone needs a teacher, a student, and a friend in their lives. As Christians, we may say that we all need a Paul, a Timothy, and a Barnabas. We each need to be learning, teaching, and loving at all times. That's how we grow. Now, I'm a natural teacher, so that part is no problem for me. And I love to read and sit with people who are further along in their journey than I am, so that part is easy. But I've already told you that I struggle with the social part of the Wheel of Life. If I'm not intentional about it, I'll end up only spending time with my family and the people I work with.

Every Wednesday morning for the past fourteen years, unless I'm out of town, I sit at a conference room table at 7:00 a.m. with my twelve closest friends. We call it our Eagle's Group. We spend an hour and a half talking, checking in with each other, studying Scripture, or reading a book together. Over the past fourteen years, I've shared everything with these men. They know me almost as well as my wife does. I get a lot of criticism and hate mail from strangers, and that doesn't faze me a bit. But if one of those guys says something or corrects me, then it's serious. That nearly carries the same weight as if Sharon said it. That's accountability. They've invested in me and I've invested in them; they've earned the right to speak into my life. God works through that kind of community to guide, encourage, and correct us. If you want to grow as an individual, you need people like that in your life.

MARRIAGE: YOUR LEGACY AS A COUPLE

Wealth building in marriage is a team sport. Starting with the very first man and woman in history, the Bible says that married couples become "one flesh" (Genesis 2:24). That means if you're trying to take control of your money, get out of debt, build wealth, teach your kids about money, or do any other part of your legacy journey without your spouse, you're only operating with half your brain! This isn't about forcing your spouse to do things *your way* or using *The Legacy Journey* principles as a club to beat the other person over the head. If you're married, the goal here is to do this whole thing side by side, arm in arm, walking out God's legacy for your family as a married couple. So in a practical way, one of the best ways to safeguard your legacy is to safeguard your marriage.

A Virtuous Wife (or Husband)

No passage of Scripture has had as big an impact on my marriage or my finances as Proverbs 31:10–11: "Who can find a virtuous wife? For her worth is far above rubies. The heart of her husband safely trusts her; so he will have no lack of gain." And for you ladies, I don't think God would mind if we also read that as, "Who can find a virtuous *husband*." This passage is all about teamwork. My wife, Sharon, is wired a lot differently than I am. She sees things that I don't. God speaks to her in a different way than He speaks to me. I learned a long time ago that every time I made a decision that went against one of Sharon's *feeeeelings*, it never turned out well. God put her in my life to help keep me inside the boundary lines.

That's true in every area of our lives, and that certainly

includes financial. Now, I'm definitely the Nerd of the family. I love spreadsheets and budgets; I get excited about calculators and playing around with numbers. Sharon? Not so much. But here's what I figured out after a few years of making stupid money decisions on my own early in our marriage: Proverbs 31:10–11 is a financial principle. Read it again: "So he will have no lack of . . ." What? Gain. No lack of *gain*. That means if I want to have some of that "gain," then I need to engage my whole brain—meaning Sharon and I have to work together on these things.

The Ownership Lens

From the moment the preacher pronounces you man and wife, Scripture says that you are to "submit to one another out of reverence for Christ" (Ephesians 5:21 NIV). To me, that's a powerful call for teamwork within marriage. The message here isn't for one partner to submit to the other in the sense of giving up all of his or her dreams and blindly following whatever the other spouse wants to do. If I ever got confused about that, it would take about three seconds for Sharon to knock my head back on straight—possibly with a frying pan. It's not about making one partner superior to the other; it's about bowing down together before the Lord. It's about recognizing as a team that we don't own anything and that God's made us—our family—responsible for a portion of *His* wealth.

When you and your spouse believe together, as a couple, that God owns it all, that changes the whole tone of the conversation about money. You can trust each other's motives because you're both asking the same question: "What is God telling us to do with these resources?" That takes the potential for selfishness out of the equation. You're not always wondering if he's angling for a new car or if she's secretly planning an unbudgeted vacation. I've talked to thousands of couples over the years who seem to bring a four-year-old's behaviors into a thirty-year marriage. That kind of selfishness steals the nobility in a marriage. It will ruin the relationship and rob you of your legacy. But when you lay your "rights" down together, all of a sudden, all of that stuff starts to go away, because money isn't all about "me, me, me" anymore. Money isn't even about "us" anymore; it's about becoming faithful managers.

The Magnification Lens

We've already said that more money simply magnifies who you already are. That definitely applies to marriage as well. So if you start with a loving, supportive marriage, the wealth you'll build over time will be a huge blessing to you and your family. A long time ago, when I was struggling to get back on my feet after the bankruptcy, I talked to a wealthy older man who had just gotten back from vacation. He was so excited because he had just spent two weeks with the people who meant the most to him. This guy took his whole family—kids, grandkids, and even his in-laws—on a two-week, all-expenses-paid, luxury ski vacation. He paid for the airplane tickets, the chalet, the ski lift tickets, the food—everything. He told me it was the most fun he and his wife had ever had. Hearing him talk about his wife of more than four decades touched me. I could tell that this man was more in love with his wife at this point in their lives than he ever had been. It was obvious that this had been a wonderful, loving couple when they were young and broke, and the wealth they'd built over the years magnified the quality of their marriage. As a young man with a wife and three little kids at the time, this gave me something to shoot for. From that point on, I dreamed of what Sharon and I could do together if we worked as a team to build our legacy.

Sadly, the opposite is true too. If your marriage is struggling and you've got cracks in your foundation, then more money will simply widen the gap. I talk to so many men whose marriages need work. They say things like, "Dave, if I just made more money, we'd be so much closer." No, they wouldn't. People like to blame a lack of money for the problems in their marriages, but that's almost never the reason for the underlying issues. Sure, money fights and financial stress are the leading causes of divorce in North America, but I think that has more to do with how couples *handle* their money than how much money they do or don't have. That's a measure of their *teamwork*, not their assets.

The bottom line is that you can't heal a wounded marriage with money. In fact, money will destroy a wounded marriage. The wealth won't create new joy; it will only magnify the problems. Have you ever known a married couple who seems to become less happy and more critical of each other the wealthier they become? I have. In the end, it turns into a nasty divorce with a team of lawyers on each side fighting for the biggest share of the wealth that ultimately drove them apart. The wealth didn't cause the divorce; their broken marriage was just revealed as the wealth grew.

No matter where you are in your wealth building, if you're married, I want you to stop right now and seriously examine your marriage. Are there cracks in the foundation? Does it feel like you and your spouse are growing further apart each year, despite your financial progress? If so, you need help. The most important piece of financial advice I can give you is to get yourselves to a counselor or your pastor's office immediately. Don't let money drive you further apart. Remember, your wealth comes from and ultimately belongs to God. Don't let His financial blessings drive a wedge through your marriage. Faithful stewardship means taking care of your family—especially your marriage—first.

The Community Lens

One way to safeguard your marriage and your legacy is to maintain quality relationships with other couples. The key word here is *quality*. What we tell our children is true: You really do become like the people you hang around with. That's actually a biblical principle. Proverbs 13:20 says, "He who walks with the wise grows wise, but a companion of fools suffers harm" (NIV). When it comes to walking with the wise, I recommend you and your spouse nurture two different types of couple relationships.

First, you should nurture spiritually healthy relationships at your financial level. That absolutely does not mean you should force some kind of wealth or income requirement on your circle of friends! I'm simply saying that we need people in our lives who understand the unique challenges and opportunities we face as we hit certain wealth milestones. When your net worth tops $1 or $2 million, for example, you'll have different estate planning issues than you used to have. It helps to have a peer group to bounce some ideas off of. Or if you're just starting to figure out your ratios for lifestyle, extra giving, and extra investing, it would be good to talk to a couple who has already been through that. These kinds of relationships can keep you from feeling isolated or, even worse, ashamed of your success. You always want to have friends around you who don't make you feel embarrassed about the fact that you're winning with money.

Second, you need to maintain your relationships with your old friends, regardless of where they are in their legacy journey. Old friends keep us grounded. These are the people who knew you when you were young and stupid. Sharon and I have friends at all different levels of wealth. Some of these couples walked with us through the bankruptcy and were instrumental in my faith walk as a new Christian. I'd never dream of leaving these friends behind! They mean the world to me, and their friendship has been a blessing to me and my family for decades. They loved us when we were broke, and they aren't impressed by our wealth now. You need these friends in your life to maintain a healthy, balanced view of your success.

CHILDREN: YOUR LEGACY AS A FAMILY

Whenever I think about what it looks like to pass down a family legacy to my children, I always think about a conversation Jesus had in Luke 9. You know the story: Jesus says to someone, "Follow Me." And the man replies, "Lord, let me first go and bury my father" (9:59). That seems like a reasonable request to me. I mean, we're called to honor our mother and father, so giving this young man time to pay his final respects to his dying father is a good and proper thing to do, right? That's why I was confused for years about Jesus' response to this basic, perfectly understandable request. Jesus replies, "Let the dead bury their own dead" (Luke 9:60). He basically tells the guy no. Ouch. That always seemed harsh to me. Why didn't Jesus let this guy bury his dad?

That's how I looked at that passage for years, until I heard Larry Burkett teach it. According to Larry, the Jewish culture had a much different view of these things than we do. When we hear, "Let me bury my father," we naturally assume that the man's father is either dead or dying. We empathize with his grief and want to comfort and console him. But, according to Burkett, that's not what was happening here. Based on Jewish culture at that time, this young man was probably saying his father was retiring—he most likely wasn't sick at all. In the Jewish tradition, an old man would turn his wealth over to his eldest son before his death, and then the son would be responsible for managing the money and taking care of his parents and any unmarried siblings. This wasn't about actually burying his father; it was about a transfer of wealth. The father's death could still have been years away at this point. That's why Jesus said no.

This passage makes me wonder, though, what it would look like if we had that kind of tradition today. If you knew that after decades of hard work, after all those years of careful wealth building, after everything you've done to build your personal and financial legacy, if you'd have to hand it all over to your kids *while you were still alive* and trust them to take care of you, how would it change the way you teach them about money? I don't know about you, but if I knew my golden years were completely dependent on my kids, I'm going to make sure they're financial geniuses! I'm going to teach them how to handle money as though my life depended on it, because guess what? Your legacy actually *does* depend on it.

The Ownership Lens

Without a proper view of God's ownership, your kids could feel like they've won the lottery if you leave them a pile of money someday. If that's the case, then that wealth will be a curse on them, and whatever legacy you've tried to build throughout your life will come to a screeching halt. That's because preparing your children to carry that legacy forward is a huge part of your legacy journey. This is so important that we'll spend most of the next chapter talking about it. For now, though, I want to impress on you that more is caught than taught. Your kids are watching you. They're going to do what you do. If they see you budgeting, saving, working, and giving, then that's what they'll most likely do. If they see you stress out about money, buy big things on impulse, go into debt for purchases, and never give a dime to anyone, then that's probably what they'll do. The best way to teach them a healthy view of God's ownership is to *show* them. You do that by the way you live your life.

But you can't just *do* these things; you have to talk about them too. The most powerful way to teach your children anything is to tell them *and* show them. They have to see that your actions and your instructions line up. Scripture says:

> These commandments that I give you today are to be on your hearts. Impress them on your children. Talk about them when you sit at home and when you walk along the road, when you lie down and when you get up. Tie them as symbols on your hands and bind them on

your foreheads. Write them on the doorframes of your houses and on your gates. (Deuteronomy 6:6–9 NIV)

That's a call to consistency and integrity in your parenting. These things have to be in your heart, in your actions, and in your words. Your home has to represent all the things you want your children to learn. It's up to you. God calls parents to be the primary mentors and teachers for their children. It's not the school's job or the church's job; teaching your kids a sense of God's ownership is your job.

When our kids were growing up, we tried our best to model the lessons God was teaching us, but we didn't do it perfectly. In the early days, we were more concerned with paying the light bill than teaching the kids anything. But we always looked for teachable moments. For example, one day I was paying bills at the kitchen table, and my oldest—eight years old at the time—asked me what I was doing. I told her, and then I took it a step further and got her to write out the check for the utility bill. She started to write the amount for the power bill, and she looked up at me with these huge, shocked eyes and said, "Dad! Electricity costs $200?" From then on, that child was always running from room to room, turning light switches off! Even though it wasn't costing her any of her own money, she felt a sense of responsibility for managing the cost of electricity in our home. She became a steward of someone else's resources; that's what a healthy view of God's ownership is all about!

The Magnification Lens

We've said that money magnifies who and what you already are. That's definitely true for your children too. Proverbs tells us to "Train up a child in the way he should go, and when he is old he will not depart from it" (Proverbs 22:6). The challenge for parents is not only to teach your kids God's ways of handling money, but to also do it in a way that resonates with their natural bent. Every child is wired a certain way. As a new dad, I was surprised to see how much unique personality my kids displayed at such a young age. Sharon and I discovered pretty quickly that we had one who was extremely organized, one who was a little wild (like her dad), and one who was super sensitive. It's hard to see the uniqueness when you're looking at someone else's kids, but you can't miss it in your own.

Those individual traits are part of who they are; that doesn't change much over time. For example, our youngest child, Daniel, has always had a servant's heart. Even as a little boy, he was always looking for ways to serve other people. Sharon and I knew that was part of his wiring, so we did our best to "train him up" with that in mind. Like all our kids, Daniel had to save up money to buy his own car. All three kids worked hard, saved as much as they could, and then we matched their savings. We called it our 401DAVE program. We told all three kids about this plan at the same time, and since Daniel is the youngest, he had the longest time to save. Because he's a hard worker and isn't a natural spender, he managed to save up a whopping $12,000 on his own. That means, after the match we promised, he was sitting on $24,000 cash at sixteen years old! I sat down with him when I gave him the match and told him that I was proud of him, but there was no way I could let a sixteen-year-old kid buy a $24,000 car. He had already found a great $14,000 Jeep he liked, so he bought the Jeep and put the other $10,000 in the bank.

A while after that, there was a horrible earthquake in Peru, close to where Daniel had been on a mission trip years earlier. He loved his time there, and he felt a special connection to the people he had met. So, when he heard about the earthquake and the great need in that community, Daniel told me he wanted to send his $10,000 to the relief efforts. Can you believe that? A sixteen-year-old young man chose to send $10,000 of his own, hard-earned money to earthquake relief. I said something like, "Daniel, that's a lot of money. You'll be heading to college soon. Are you sure you want to give your money away?"

He replied matter-of-factly, "But Dad, it's not my money. It's God's money. That's what you taught us, right?" Sharon and I were blown away (and more than a little humbled), but as it sank in, his response made perfect sense. He was wired to be a servant and giver, and Sharon and I had done our best to teach him about working, saving, and God's ownership. That put him in a position to do something at sixteen that most adults can never do: give $10,000 away—and with a smile. That's the magnification principle at work: Because of his hard work, he had wealth to share. That wealth simply magnified what was already there.

The Community Lens

Getting the community lens right with your children is absolutely crucial. You can spend all day every day with them for the first fifteen years of their lives, teaching them the Bible, walking with them through each stage of life, showing them what it takes to be a mature, valuable member of society. But if you don't step back and look at the bigger community around them, all of your hard work can be undone in the blink of an eye. The apostle Paul put it this way: "Evil company corrupts good habits" (1 Corinthians 15:33). You and I might say, "You become who you hang around with." We know this is true for adults, but it is so much more powerful for children—especially teenagers. I cannot stress this enough: You've got to know your kids' friends. That means you have to be involved and know what their friends are into.

This used to drive my kids crazy. Rachel—the more dramatic one—always used to argue with me when I told her to stay away from certain friends. She'd say, "Dad, I'm sixteen years old. I know what I stand for. I can hang around with them and be okay." But then, slowly but surely, she'd start coming home with new bad habits—nothing major, just things like being a little disrespectful to her mom or trying to bend the rules a bit. As soon as we noticed it, we cut her off from the source. I didn't have anything against her friends, but as her parent, I was not going to allow outside influences to turn her into something I knew she wasn't—whether or not she understood it at the time. Some of you may need to grow a backbone about this. No matter how much they start to look like adults, your teenagers are still growing up. It's up to you to steer them in the right direction, and that includes helping them identify bad influences that could ultimately wreck their lives.

And while we're at it, I want to encourage you to examine your own friends. Don't tell your children to stay away from bad influences if you aren't doing it too. The psalmist says, "Blessed is the one who does not walk in step with the wicked or stand in the way that sinners take or sit in the company of mockers" (Psalm 1:1 NIV). Even as an adult, you can get knocked off course by your messed-up friends just as easily as your kids can. Even worse, you could bring those bad influences into your children's lives. Don't let your own choices in friends destroy your family legacy.

Getting these messages to your children at a young age is so important that my daughter Rachel and I have written a book that talks about all of these things in more detail. If you still have kids in the house, you should check out *Smart Money Smart Kids*. Teaching your kids how and why to work, spend, save, and give throughout their lives is one of the most important things you could ever do to guarantee a legacy that lasts. Like the Proverb says, "The righteous man walks in his integrity; his children are blessed after him" (Proverbs 20:7).

No Kids? No Problem.

If you don't have kids, you just need to redefine what US means for you in the legacy journey framework. Maybe it's investing in nieces and nephews. Maybe it's getting involved in a children's ministry, working with an orphanage, or financially supporting a family seeking to adopt. No matter what it is, I encourage you to talk to God about how He wants to use you to impact the next generation. You want a legacy that goes somewhere, so be intentional about finding ways the good work you're doing today can bless others later.

OTHER RELATIONSHIPS: YOUR LEGACY EXTENDED

We've talked about how to safeguard ourselves as individuals, our marriages, and our children from the challenges that wealth can bring into our lives. That's a great start, but we're still left with how the legacy we're building can affect other relationships. The truth is, your personal wealth can have an unexpected impact on your extended family and friends. I've seen so many people caught off guard by this. They spend years or decades focusing on their legacy, only to have it torn apart by toxic relationships they weren't prepared for. To truly safeguard your legacy, you've got to take a good, hard look at the people around you and set some boundaries to protect yourself—and those relationships.

The Ownership and Magnification Lenses

I guarantee you, no matter how great your family and friends are, no matter how much you think I'm exaggerating, you will have people in your circle who think you owe them money just because they're in your life. That's where the magnification lens comes in because your success may reveal the true characters of your friends and family members. As your wealth grows, some of these people will get bolder and bolder in making demands about how you should "help" them. We've said a few times that grown children sometimes feel like they've hit the jackpot when they receive their inheritance from wealthy parents, but sometimes the roles get reversed. I talk to successful young adults all the time whose parents have started making demands on them just because they "can afford it" or because "I'm your mother." It's heartbreaking because it puts a burden of guilt over someone's success, and it puts an adult child in the position of enabling a parent's bad behavior. That's a totally toxic situation.

This is an entitlement issue, whether it's coming from your children, your parents, your best friend, or your fourth cousin twice removed. Yes, we're called to honor our parents. Yes, we're called to take care of our families before we do anything else with money. But that doesn't mean we *owe* anyone anything. If your mother is a cocaine addict, giving her money is the last thing you should do. That's not helping her. If your child refuses to grow up and get a job, supporting him financially is a complete waste of money because it's only keeping him from getting out there and doing what God's called him to do. If your best friend is up to her eyeballs in debt because she's an out-of-control shopaholic, paying off her credit card bills won't be a blessing. It will just wipe out the symptom while ignoring the behaviors that got her into trouble. This means you're going to have to get comfortable setting—and enforcing—clear boundaries in some of these relationships. *Boundaries* is a scary word for many people, but they are a crucial part of safeguarding your legacy. You must be intentional about setting boundaries in your relationships, and you, your friends, and your family members need to know when something falls out-of-bounds.

How you respond in all of these situations is an ownership issue. Remember, this is God's money, so you have to keep asking yourself, *Is this how God would want me to spend His resources?* Scripture says, "The blessing of the LORD makes one rich, and He adds no sorrow with it" (Proverbs 10:22). That tells me that God doesn't want us putting His wealth into a sorrowful situation. That won't be a blessing to anyone. When you find yourself caught in someone's twisted web of entitlement, just take yourself out of the equation. Then ask yourself this one question: Is this a situation that God would pour His blessings into? If the answer is yes, then maybe it's something He wants you to do with His money. If the answer is obviously no, then run!

The Community Lens

The point here is not to be scared and freaked out about the people in your life. Yes, you're going to have some people around you who get twisted up and confused by your success. That hurts when it happens, but it's not your fault. You can't be responsible for how other people behave. What you can do, though, is make sure you surround yourself with quality friends who help you navigate through this mess. When we talked about marriage, I suggested you find some friends at your wealth level. That's your new financial peer group because you're all going through these unique challenges together. That comes into play with your extended family and friends too. You need people in your life who are going through the same things with their own crazy relatives! You can lean on each other and learn from each other. You don't have to go through this alone!

A LEGACY IN RELATIONSHIPS

I talk to so many people who are only concerned about the math, the practical and tactical side of wealth building. That part is easy! There's no big secret to building wealth. It just takes time, patience, and wisdom. Sure, there's plenty to learn about investments (which we'll cover in "The Pinnacle Point," the bonus chapter in the back of this book). But what most people overlook is the fact that our relationships have as much or more impact on our wealth and legacy than our investment strategy does. You can do smart things with money your whole life and leave millions of dollars when you die, but if you have sick, weak, toxic relationships all around you, that wealth won't make it to your children's children. It will not only disappear, but it will also destroy your family along the way.

Years ago, a guy called into my radio show to talk about his mother's nursing home selection. She was a godly woman in her late eighties who had been widowed for twenty years at that point. She and her late husband never had a big income. Their family never had much, and honestly, they never really even thought about teaching their children about money. They never had those conversations around the dinner table. They were simple country folks who did the best they could with what they had, and they had done okay. Now, as she entered the season of life that required full-time care, she was almost ninety years old with $200,000 in the bank—enough to at least have a choice in the quality of care she could receive through her final years. But this guy's call made my jaw drop. He was calling to ask me how he could talk his mother into choosing a cheaper nursing home because he was afraid the one she picked would eat up his inheritance! Can you believe that? This middle -aged man was more concerned about how much he'd get than he was about how well his mother would be treated in the few years she had left. He was acting like that money was already his, and it bugged him that she'd *dare* to spend *his money* on her healthcare. That kind of attitude makes me sick. It's a toxic form of entitlement that, sadly, characterizes too many families.

Now, contrast that to another story. I have a good friend who came from a family that talked about money. His parents weren't wealthy, but they were intentional about teaching their kids the kinds of things we've been talking about in this book. They worked hard, saved, planned, and gave generously, and they made sure they lived these principles out in front of their children. My buddy lost his mother several years ago, and he and his dad have grown even closer in the years since then. As my friend grew his business, he started doing pretty well financially. He lived like his parents taught him to, always saving, always giving. Then, a few years ago, my friend did something he'd dreamed of doing for years: He wrote a check and paid off his dad's house! How cool is that? That's the kind of stuff you can do—and want to do—when you come from a family that is intentional about protecting their relationships when it comes to money.

Remember what we read earlier from Deuteronomy: "I call heaven and earth as witnesses today against you, that I have set before you life and death, blessing and cursing; therefore choose life, that both you and your descendants may live" (30:19). Having these conversations with your family and friends, working together to protect your marriage, making sure you're taking care of yourself mentally and spiritually . . . these are life and death decisions when it comes to money. Your wealth has the power to bless your family or completely tear it apart. The guy who was more concerned with money than he was his own mother's well-being? That family chose cursing. But my friend who used his wealth to show his love and appreciation for his dad? Clearly, that family chose blessing a long time ago. That's my hope for you too.

CHAPTER SEVEN

Generational Legacy

Bologna and tomato sandwiches.

Crazy as it sounds, that's one of the most powerful, meaningful memories I have from my college years: sitting at my grandparents' kitchen table eating bologna and tomato sandwiches with Grandpaw. When I was growing up, my grandparents lived only a couple of hours away, so I certainly knew them and had spent time with them. But it wasn't until I went to college and moved near them that I really got to know them as a young adult. They lived in Alcoa, Tennessee, just outside of Knoxville where I went to college. I'd often run over to their house for lunch between classes or for dinner some nights when I just needed a home-cooked meal. And hey, I was a broke college student, and they had free food!

Grandpaw worked for Alcoa Aluminum for thirty-eight years as their head cost accountant. He had a brilliant mind for numbers; maybe I got just a little bit of that from him. I guess when you're a kid, you kind of have a *sense* that your grandparents actually have a life outside of their role as grandparents, but most of us don't stop to think about that. However, during those great conversations I had with Grandpaw at his kitchen table, I realized what an amazing man he really was. We talked about family and relationships. We talked about money. We talked about business. He had this great way of tying it all together, and it always felt like one conversation flowed perfectly into the next. He was a great, great man.

Scripture says, "A good man leaves an inheritance to his children's children" (Proverbs 13:22). Clearly, the Bible teaches us to leave an inheritance for future generations. My grandfather left me an inheritance of character and of wonderful memories. Sure, a big part of that inheritance is a legacy of love— the memories I have of my grandfather are precious to me. They are a big part of the man I've become, and I wouldn't trade them for anything in the world! But I also think Scripture makes it clear that we're called to manage God's resources well so that we can leave a financial legacy too. There's a biblical model for passing wealth generationally, and there are practical things we can do to make sure our legacy not only survives but also increases as it moves down to our kids, grandkids, and great-grandkids. We're going to take a serious look at that in this chapter, as we get our hands dirty with some practical and tactical things we should be doing today to create a financial legacy that lasts.

A GOOD MAN . . .

We've already talked a lot about Proverbs 13:22. That verse sets the tone for *The Legacy Journey*. That's the goal, right? We want to focus on doing things today that impact our children, our grandchildren, our great-grandchildren, and beyond. What would it look like if we actually lived our lives like we believe this verse?

Anyone Can Do It

Anyone in America can retire a millionaire. That's a bold statement, I know. If you've never read any of my other books or taken our *Financial Peace University* class, then that might even be a shocking statement. Let me tell you why it sounds so surprising: It's because we get hit nonstop with all kinds of messages from our culture that tell us we can't do it. I've heard them all: "I just can't find a job." "The little man can't get ahead." "The system is rigged." I even have a relative who just walks around yelling, "The corporations! It's the corporations!" I have no idea what he means, but in his mind, "the corporations" are the reason why he can't win with money. Personally, I think most of these excuses are garbage.

I know that it can be hard finding a job, and I know the economy has some wild ups and downs. I get that. I didn't say it's *easy* to become a millionaire; I just said anyone can do it. If you learned God's ways of handling money and used them throughout your life, if you stayed out of debt, if you saved for emergencies, if you planned and invested for the future, and if you did that consistently over time, where would you end up? You'd be wealthy. Did you know that practically any twenty-five-year-old person could end up with more than $1 million by retirement without breaking a sweat? Do the math. If you invest just $100 a month in a decent growth stock mutual fund from age twenty-five to age sixty-five, you'd have more than $1 million! And that's just with a hundred bucks a month! If a million is what you had at retirement, you could live pretty well just on the growth without ever touching the principal. That means you'd have $1 million to pass down generationally.

Let's not stop there. Let's say you did that, and more importantly, you taught your children to do that. If you have two kids, imagine them retiring at age sixty-five with $1 million each. That $2 million plus twenty years' worth of growth on the $1 million you left would come to almost $12 million combined! Take this same thing down one more generation—to your grandchildren—and we're looking at a financial legacy in the neighborhood of $100–200 million! What could your family do for the kingdom of God generationally if you started the ball rolling? What if you gave them not just money, but also the character and wisdom to actually do this stuff? And again, that's with only $100 a month. Just imagine what this would look like if you actually did what we teach and invested 15 percent of your income into retirement!

So Why Don't Most People Do This?

If this is possible for practically every single family in America, why on earth don't people actually do it? I think we see the answer in Proverbs 21:20: "In the house of the wise are stores of choice food and oil, but a foolish man devours all he has" (NIV). Wise people save money, delay pleasure, and make sacrifices for their families. Foolish people blow all their money on fancy cars, exotic vacations, and expensive jewelry they can't really afford. They're more concerned about themselves—what they want and what they can do to impress other people. For too many, it's all about me, me, me. What I want. What I can consume. What I can buy. Sometimes you meet these people and it's like they think the axis of the world runs right through the top of their head. They talk and act as though the whole world revolves around them. And in our culture today, we sometimes even celebrate that kind of selfishness. We make jokes about it, and we slap bumper stickers on our luxury cars that say, "I'm spending my kids' inheritance." That's not funny to me; it's sad, and I don't think it's biblically wise. I think that's just another way of telling the world, "I don't care about future generations, because it's all about me." It's a sad statement about the maturity level of many Americans.

That's definitely not who I want to be. I want to be the grandfather or great-grandfather who changed his family tree forever. I want to be old man Rockefeller, the first generation to draw a line in the sand and say, "I can do better. My family can do better. And from this point forward, we will." There's nothing wrong with nice things and enjoying your success; we've covered that at length already. But you can never put nice things above the legacy you're leaving for your family.

THE BIBLICAL MODEL FOR
GENERATIONAL WEALTH

All through the Bible I see wealthy families passing down their wealth to future generations. I believe Scripture shows us that godly families are called to manage wealth for God's glory. The responsibility for managing God's resources doesn't end when the head of the household dies; that responsibility is passed along with the wealth. It's not a surprise, and it's not a Hail Mary pass at the deathbed. It should be the result of a lifetime of conversations with your children about how to manage that wealth for the kingdom of God. That's the calling God's put on the family, and that's the responsibility your children take on when they accept their role as heirs.

Your Children's Children

Generational wealth is not about materialism or consumption. It's about taking responsibility—as a family over several generations—for managing the wealth that God's put in your care. Building up wealth just so your kids never have to work is not biblical. Warren Buffet says, "A very rich person should leave his kids enough to do anything but not enough to do nothing." We're *all* called to godly work and productivity. Proverbs 10:4 says, "Lazy hands make for poverty, but diligent hands bring wealth" (NIV). The Bible never says that one generation should work hard so the following generations can take it easy! Instead, we see every generation building on the hard work and success of the previous one.

That's the story of Abraham and his son Isaac. Abraham was an extremely wealthy man. Genesis 24:1 says that God blessed Abraham "in every way," and that certainly included wealth. In verse 35, Abraham's servant explains, "The LORD has blessed my master abundantly, and he has become wealthy. He has given him sheep and cattle, silver and gold, male and female servants, and camels and donkeys" (NIV). Translation: Abraham was loaded! And what happened to that wealth after Abraham died? Genesis 25:5 says, "Abraham left everything he owned to Isaac" (NIV). Scripture shows that Abraham was generous throughout his life, but he still maintained his wealth so that he could pass it on to his son.

What was the result of that generational transfer? Genesis 25:11 says, "After Abraham's death, God blessed his son Isaac" (NIV). So Abraham saved and built wealth throughout his life, and then he passed it to his son. Isaac received that wealth and added to it through God's blessing. In Genesis 26:3, God says to Isaac, "I will be with you and will bless you. For to you and your descendants I will give all these lands and will confirm the oath I swore to your father Abraham" (NIV). Verses 12 through 13 of that same chapter show us how big that blessing really was to the second generation: "Isaac planted crops in that land and the same year reaped a hundredfold, because the LORD blessed him. The man became rich, and his wealth continued to grow until he became very wealthy" (NIV).

During Israel's long journey to the Promised Land, the call for families to pass down their wealth to family heirs was outright mandated. Speaking for the Lord, Moses commands the Israelites, "No inheritance shall change hands from one tribe to another, but every tribe of the children of Israel shall keep its own inheritance" (Numbers 36:9). Isn't that interesting? Each tribe's inheritance had to be passed down the family line, and they were prevented from sharing it with the other tribes. No wealth redistribution going on here.

And let's not forget about Job. We always talk about Job as being the guy who went through unbelievable hardships—and he did. I never want to go through *any* of what he did. But what we often lose in that story is how richly God *blessed* Job too. There are some inferences in Scripture that make me think Job may have been the wealthiest man on the planet at that time.

But then Job lost everything, and I mean everything. He lost his wealth, his home, his family, his kids, his friends . . . everything. There was nothing left except a pile of garbage to sit on and a few clueless buddies ready to give him some bad advice.

What happened to Job at the end of the story? God showed up, and He restored everything several times over. Job 42:12 says, "Now the LORD blessed the latter days of Job more than his beginning; for he had fourteen thousand sheep, six thousand camels, one thousand yoke of oxen, and one thousand female donkeys." That's a *lot*. And here's what I like: "In all the land were found no women so beautiful as the daughters of Job; and their father gave them an inheritance among their brothers" (Job 42:15). Now this was in a time when the daughters got nothing; everything was passed to the men. But Job's wealth was so big, and he loved his family so much, he went against tradition and passed his wealth on to *all* his children. Speaking as the father of two girls myself, I can't imagine doing anything else either.

Probably one of the greatest examples of generational wealth transfer is King David. Most of us picture David as a little shepherd kid in the story of David and Goliath, with old King Saul's armor hanging off his skinny frame. It's easy to forget that David went on to some pretty big things after that. He was a great king, and he had plans to build a massive temple for God. But then he got himself into a bit of trouble, and God removed David's right to build the temple. Instead, the assignment was given to David's son, Solomon.

I have a friend who is a brilliant economist, and he dug into the description of the temple in 2 Chronicles. Once he factored in all the gold, woodwork, and incredible craftsmanship and décor, my friend estimated that Solomon's temple would have cost about $21 billion in today's dollars. That's *billion* with a "b." Where do you think that money came from? Solomon used *David's money* to build the temple, so that would mean that David and Solomon were billionaires! And the part I really like is that Solomon didn't just receive David's *money*; he received David's *responsibility* as well. That's what we've been saying throughout this book: Godly stewards don't just pass along wealth to future generations; they also pass along the responsibility for managing it for God's glory. I believe that's the biblical model for generational wealth.

A 501(c)(3) Is Not Holier Than Your Children

Sometimes wealthy people fall into the trap of thinking the "holy" thing to do with their money is to leave it all to a non-profit organization, often categorized as a 501(c)(3) for tax purposes. We hear those messages all the time, don't we? We look at the amazing things that people like Bill Gates are doing with their money, and we applaud them for their generosity. I want to be crystal clear here: I think Bill Gates is doing some incredible things, and there's no question that he is going to go down in history as one of the most generous, most giving, most world-changing figures in modern history. But I still disagree with part of his plan. He's gone on record saying that his plan is for most of his wealth to be completely spent within twenty years of his and his wife's death. On the surface, that may sound like a good or generous thing—and it is. The problem is, though, one of the biggest personal fortunes in the history of the world will totally vanish within one generation. Even though the money will be spent in wonderful ways, it will still be gone forever.

There's even a growing amount of political pressure to make sure family wealth never makes it to the second generation. One prominent billionaire and political activist recently went on record saying he thinks the government should continue to increase the estate tax to give people a greater incentive to leave more of their wealth to nonprofits. It's kind of funny that this is coming from a guy who inherited his billions from previous generations. If he really believes that, maybe he could prove it by giving all he has away to nonprofits today. He won't, of course, which makes him a hypocrite, or at the very least, someone who just likes to hear himself talk. Again, though, well-run nonprofits are great if they line up with your values and you choose to contribute to their causes. But there should never be pressure—social, political, or spiritual—to leave everything to one, and there definitely shouldn't be tax laws put in place to force people to do it.

I just don't see that kind of "use it or lose it" attitude about wealth and giving in the Bible. Instead, I see example after example of godly families passing down their wealth—and the management (stewardship) of that wealth—to future generations. As that happens, the wealth grows and more and more people are blessed over several generations. Why do we think it's better to give everything to a nonprofit than to entrust it to the children we've spent decades training? I've seen some nonprofits that are *terrible* at managing money; why should a 501(c)(3) classification make that a better choice at managing my wealth for the kingdom than my own children?

If your kids are functional, know how and why to manage money God's ways, love Jesus, and aren't confused about the responsibility of wealth, then they should be first in line to carry this financial blessing into the next generation—even above a well-run nonprofit. If you're passionate about a particular charity or ministry and trust the way they manage their money, then by all means make that a part of your plan; just don't make it the entire plan. But a broke nonprofit? That shouldn't even be an option. Your money will be wasted faster and potentially do more damage in a poorly run 501(c)(3) than it would in almost any other situation.

Nonprofits Are Not Anointed

Since I will be misunderstood, let me say it one more time: I am not against leaving your wealth to a nonprofit or your church (unless they are poorly run). I just want you to be freed from the toxic and false message that you should give your money to a "holy" organization rather than leave it to a functional, godly family. Nonprofits are not by definition "holy." And leaving your money to your family is neither selfish nor unholy. That is simply wrong.

Keep in mind, God did not anoint nonprofits; the IRS did. Prior to the tax code being put in place in the last century, there was no such thing as a nonprofit organization. Sure, there were churches and charities, but the word *nonprofit* didn't really exist. This is an IRS designation, not a biblical designation.

PRACTICAL ESTATE PLANNING

Okay, we've talked about the biblical model for passing wealth generationally, and it's clear that I believe it's both moral and biblical to build wealth with a goal of leaving it to responsible, godly heirs to further bless future generations. So let's switch gears and look at some practical things that need to be part of your estate plan. Whenever I bring this up, I always get someone who says, "But, Dave, if I talk about doing a will . . . I'll die!" Well, guess what? My team has done extensive research on the subject, and we've found with 100 percent certainty that you are, in fact, going to die. We all are. Humanity has a 100 percent mortality rate. With that in mind, let's make sure we're doing the right things now so our families won't have to deal with a huge estate crisis later in the middle of their grief.

Raise Great Adults

I recently heard my friend, author Andy Andrews, talk about parenting. He said something that really stuck in my head because it lined up with how Sharon and I raised our three kids. He said, "I'm not that interested in raising great kids. I'm more interested in raising pretty good kids who grow up to be great adults." If you're focused only on having great kids, your parenting style will be all about basic rule following and stiff punishment for going out of bounds. Your kids will be well-mannered and polite, and you may have the picture of the perfect family. At least until they go to college. Then, these little robots you controlled for eighteen years will go crazy with rebellion, getting a degree in beer pong, and that will do more to shape who they become as adults than anything you did.

Now, there were definitely rules in place in the Ramsey house, and my kids knew what it meant to get a swat on the behind or spend a week or two grounded when they messed up. But that can't be all you do. If your goal is to raise kids who become great adults, you have to give them room to grow

—and that means giving them the responsibility to manage some stuff and the freedom to fail. You want your kids to make their biggest mistakes while they're still under your roof. If your goal is to leave a huge financial legacy to the next generation, you have to make sure your kids have the maturity and character to manage that wealth wisely for the Lord. If you get this right, the wealth you leave them will truly be a blessing; if you get it wrong, your wealth will completely destroy their lives. Make sure you're doing all you can to prepare the next generation to shoulder the responsibility you'll leave them one day.

You Need a Will

Sometimes it seems like I can't write a book or go one day on the radio without talking about the need for everyone over the age of eighteen to have a will. I talk about this over and over and over again, and I will until every adult in America gets the message: You need a will—today!

"But Dave, I don't have any wealth or big possessions. Why do I need a will?" Because a will does a lot more than just say who gets what. Besides, even if you only have one big thing like a home, it could take months or even years for a court to figure out what to do with it. There's just no point in that! And if you have young kids, don't even try to rationalize not having a will. A will outlines your plans for your children in detail, so there's no question where they go or what happens to them. Do you want the state to determine that? For all you know, the state could put your children in the care of your craziest relative. Don't put your children in the court's hands. Love them enough to spell out your wishes for them in a will.

Keep in mind that wills are state-specific. You can't get one boilerplate will that works the same all over the US Probate and estate-planning laws are governed by the state, not the federal government, so it changes from state to state. That means if you move to another state, you need to update your will. Even if you don't move out of state, you should still carefully review your will every couple of years to make sure it still reflects your current wealth level, possessions, and wishes.

One big objection people have to doing a will is the basic hassle factor. I'm not going to lie to you: Doing a will is not fun. The legal part of it is dry and boring, and then there's the emotional part. To do your will right, you have to seriously think about dying. Who wants to do that? Well, your kids want you to think about it and plan for it, because if you don't think about it now, you'll leave them in a mess later. One thing that makes this easier for married couples is what's called a mirror-image will. Assuming you're married and you both do the estate planning together (a necessity, by the way), then you can do a full draft of the will in one person's name and then mirror it for the other spouse. When Sharon and I did ours, we wrote everything up in my name for my will, and when we were done, the lawyer ran another copy of it but put her name in place of mine everywhere. That way, we have matching wills that reflect our wishes. It saves money and keeps you from having to figure everything out twice. Easy.

Other things that absolutely must be in your will include healthcare power of attorney, living will instructions, and child guardianship. Healthcare power of attorney states clearly who is authorized to make your healthcare decisions if you are incapacitated. So, if you're in an accident, who do you trust to make those life-saving decisions on your behalf? Put it in the will.

The living will outlines your life-ending wishes, which takes a huge amount of pressure off of your spouse or relatives. Say you're in a coma from a car wreck, and you aren't doing well. The doctors declare you brain-dead and say you'll never wake up, but they can keep you breathing on a machine for years. Is that what you want? Your living will is the place to make your wishes known. Don't force your spouse to make the decision to turn off the machines. You can make that decision yourself; you just have to make it now and put it in writing.

Child guardianship is an absolute must if you have minor kids. Like we already said, this outlines your exact instructions for who will take care of your children if you and the other parent are gone. You can name whomever you want; just get their permission first. It does not have to be a family member, but if you die without these instructions in place, the court is likely to put your children in the care of a family member, whether or not that's really the best place for them. Don't wimp out on this. Your kids are counting on you to look out for them—and that includes looking out for their needs after you're gone.

A will doesn't have to be too complicated unless you have built up a great deal of wealth. If your assets are under $1 million, you can probably get by just fine with a basic will through an attorney or online service. If you have more than $1 million, or if there are some unusual circumstances in your family or estate, then I recommend working with an estate planner to make sure you've accounted for everything. It may cost you $1000 or more, but that's a small price to pay for making sure your legacy passes to the next generation intact.

Avoid the Drama

Picture it: The lawyer's conference room. The trophy wife. The goofy stepson. The grieving family. The letter opener slicing through the thick yellow envelope. The gasps as one family member discovers he's been cut out of the inheritance. Welcome to the reading of the will—if you're watching a movie, that is.

In real life, there should be no drama involved in "the reading of the will" after you're gone. That's because grown-ups don't leave surprises and disappointments in the will that the family doesn't already know about. If you don't want your family to find out your final wishes until after you're dead, you're what's known as a coward. Grow up and get over it. In more than two decades of working with clients and people who call in to my radio show, I've heard thousands of horror stories about ticking time bombs in someone's will that blew a family apart. Think about it: There is no worse time for a person to be surprised with disappointing news than when their whole family is going through a painful loss. Emotions are already running so high that one little spark could keep siblings from talking to each other for the next thirty years. You do a will to provide for and protect your family; don't let it be the thing that tears the family apart.

Avoid this by doing the reading of the will while you're still alive. No, you don't need to make this a big dramatic event, and you don't even need to read the will word for word. But you should make sure everyone knows your wishes. Tell them who gets what. Tell them what happens with the kids. Tell them how much you want to leave to which charities. Tell them everything, and tell them yourself! Let them hear it straight from you. That one simple act can save your family years of heartache and legal battles contesting the will.

I know one sweet old guy who's kind of a fanatic about this stuff. He watched his siblings get torn apart by a surprise in their parents' will, and he was determined that his own kids and grandkids would never go through that because of him. So, if you were to walk through this guy's house today, you'd see little sticky notes with people's names on almost everything. Walking through his living room is like taking a tour of his will! I don't recommend you go quite that far, but at least love your family enough to be honest with them today. If you have kids or grandkids who are addicted to drugs and who you can't trust with money, then tell them today that they won't receive anything in the condition they're in. Who knows? That alone could be the motivation they need to get help and clean up their lives. And if they do, then by all means update your will!

A Matter of Trust

One thing that's becoming more popular in the world of estate planning lately is the living trust. Estate planners are pitching this pretty heavily inside the church too, but I'm not a fan of these arrangements at all. Here's the deal. I never recommend something to someone that I wouldn't use myself. And since a living trust makes no sense in almost any situation, I can't recommend it to you either. I'm not mad at the living trust people, and I don't think they're ripping anyone off; I just don't see any benefit to the hassle that a living trust creates. Unlike a standard will, living trusts require you to move your assets out from under your own control to a trust before your death. As a result, even basic financial decisions—like adjusting investments, managing bank accounts, giving to charities, and buying or selling real estate—have to go through a trustee because the trust legally owns everything. While it's true that larger estates require a higher level of sophistication, detail, and privacy in estate planning, a living trust probably isn't the answer in the vast majority of cases. It definitely wasn't in mine. More times than not, people in Baby Step 7 who are living and generously giving like no one else can protect their legacies through an estate plan built around a carefully designed will. And if it's a large estate, there will most likely be several trusts put in place upon death.

Despite how often the financial world pitches living trusts, there are three main problems that are hard to ignore. First, living trusts are the primary upsell in the estate-planning world. Rather than simplifying matters, living trusts create an expensive and usually unnecessary add-on to estate planning. They also require an ongoing relationship with an estate planner because you need a representative every time you want to adjust your assets.

Second, most living trusts are never fully funded. Setting up a trust is usually an expensive process, but the estate planners I've talked to say most of their clients never actually fully fund the living trust after setting it up. The hassle of retitling and redeeding everything into the name of the trust is so complicated and frustrating that only the nerdiest of the Nerds tend to follow through. But an unfunded trust isn't really a trust at all; it's just a waste of money that provides no benefit to you or your loved ones.

Third, living trusts create a cumbersome problem every time you want to do something with your investments or property. In a living trust, you don't personally own anything—the trust does. That means you can't make a move without getting the legal approval of the trustee. For example, I buy and sell real estate, review my mutual funds, and set up new investments all the time. If I had everything in a living trust, I'd have to move my estate planner and the trustee into an office next door just to handle the day-to-day operations of my estate! I just haven't seen any benefit to outweigh these issues, so I stay away from living trusts.

That said, I'm not saying that *all* trusts are bad. For example, if you have a child with special needs, you should look into a special needs trust. I have a friend whose son has Down syndrome, so they set up a special needs trust as part of their estate plan. The trust kicks in when my friend and his wife die, and a portion of his wealth will go to fund the trust. Those funds will be managed by a trustee they've named and used exclusively to care for the ongoing needs of his son for the rest of his life. That's a good thing. There are other kinds of trusts that you can put in your estate plan that don't start until after you're gone, and Sharon and I have some of this as part of our plan. The point is that all trusts are not created equally. Just move slowly, get trusted counsel, and avoid the trusts that mess with your wealth while you're still alive.

Avoiding Mr. Taxman

Federal estate tax planning may be your biggest challenge because the government puts massive taxes on estates once they reach a certain size. I want to be crystal clear here: There is absolutely nothing wrong or immoral about using every legal means available to avoid taxes. In fact, I'll take it a step further. I believe that taking advantage of every legal method of avoiding taxes is actually good stewardship. If you think that giving the government money that you don't *have* to give them is good stewardship, I question your intellect—and your sanity. I've never seen any individual, corporation, or organization waste money as quickly and effectively as the federal government. If you want to bring the kingdom-shaping power of your money to a screeching halt, then by all means, give it to the government.

I am absolutely not suggesting you do anything immoral or illegal to hide your money from taxes. You need to give the government every penny you are obligated to give them—but not one penny more. I don't need the government to redistribute the wealth God asked me to manage; God has some pretty good ideas about how to distribute it Himself. And I'll start with giving to the causes that God directs me to give to and leaving my wealth to the three children I've raised to be wise stewards of God's resources.

Till Death Do Us Part?

For years, as I've talked about these things, people have asked me, "Dave, if I'm supposed to be intentional about protecting my wealth, should I get a prenuptial agreement before I get married?" My answer has always been pretty clear. If you're getting married, you need to be able to put *everything* into the marriage. If you're not willing to do that, then you might love your stuff more than you love your future spouse. That's a problem. One day, a lady called the radio show to talk to me. She was about to get married, but her future husband wanted her to sign a prenup because he had a '67 Ford Mustang he didn't want to lose if the marriage didn't last. I told that caller exactly what I would have said to my daughters if either of their husbands had ever tried something like that. I said, "Run! This guy loves his car more than he loves you!"

The old wedding vows said, "For richer and for poorer, in sickness and in health, 'til death do us part, *unto thee all my worldly goods I pledge.*" I think that's both beautiful and right. If you're not willing to commit all that you have, you shouldn't get married. That's what I've always believed, and it's what I still believe to this day. However, after all these years of working with people at all levels of wealth, I've just recently started to make a very slight exception to that rule. If one of the people coming into the marriage has extreme assets and the other person has little to no assets, then you might consider a prenup in that situation. I'm not saying you *have* to; I'm just saying that's the only time I'd be willing to budge on my "no prenup" position.

Here's the reason: Wealth can make you a target. I've seen so much weirdness in this area. And it may not even be your future spouse who's weird; they may have weird family members or other influencers who twist the broke marriage partner into something you wouldn't have expected. But again, let's clarify what I'm talking about. This isn't about protecting a '67 Mustang; this is about someone with extreme wealth marrying someone with nothing. So if one partner is broke and the other has $2 million or more, then a prenup may make sense. Pray about it, talk about it, and get wise counsel before you make any decisions on this issue.

Don't Deed the House Before You Die
The next practical piece of estate-planning advice I want to give you is something I've seen hundreds of times, but I've never

understood. Do not deed your home to your family members prior to your death. If your parents are getting on in years, do not let them do this either. This is a nightmare situation that solves no problems and ends up costing the heirs a ton of money. This happens when someone or a couple gets the idea of transferring their home into their child's name before their death. For some reason, they think it's a wise move to go ahead and take care of the house before death so it doesn't get caught up in the will or anything. Bad, bad move.

Here's what happens: Let's say Mom and Dad bought their home in 1963 and paid $13,000 for it. If you weren't around or buying houses in 1963, you'll just have to trust me when I tell you that these are real numbers. Now, all these years later, that house they bought for $13,000 is worth $400,000. That wouldn't be unusual at all in a good neighborhood over fifty years. So Mom and Dad are sitting in a $400,000 home and decide to deed the home to their kids because someone told them it was a good idea. If Mom and Dad deed the home before death, then the kids' tax basis is the same as their parents' tax basis, which was $13,000—their original purchase price. That means the kids will have to pay capital gains tax on the difference between the $400,000 they sell it for and the $13,000 Mom and Dad originally paid for it. Basically, they have to pay capital gains tax on $387,000, which would be more than $50,000 in taxes.

However, if Mom and Dad had waited and simply left the house to the kids in their will after their death, their tax basis would be the current market value at the time of death, which is $400,000. So if the kids sell the house for $400,000, they pay zero taxes. That's how big a mistake this one move can be.

You want to leave your kids what's called the stepped-up basis of current market value, not the basis on what you originally paid for the home. That one thing can save your children tens of thousands of dollars in unnecessary taxes.

The Family Constitution

One last thing I'd encourage you to do as you work on your legacy journey is to create a family constitution. This is a document that defines your family's values, recognizes your family's dysfunctions, and considers your family's relationships. At its heart, the family constitution clearly spells out who and what your family is—and what it isn't. This is an exercise my family did several years ago, and it opened the door to all kinds of conversations for all of us. We found that there were several things we had all just assumed but had never really talked about. And there were other things that we discovered were incredibly important but had never even considered before. I have to admit, it was surprising. I've always been a big goal-setter, and, as we've talked about, one of the most powerful things you can do with goals is to simply write them down. As we worked on our family constitution, I discovered that the act of writing our values and beliefs down was just as important as writing goals. Once that piece fell into place for me, the whole thing clicked.

Because we're a family of faith, it was important for us to put the Bible at the center of our family constitution. So, at the very top of the first page is Joshua 24:15: "Choose for yourselves this day whom you will serve ... But as for me and my house, we will serve the LORD." That sets the tone for everything that follows. That's who we are as a family: We're a group of men and women who are always striving to serve the Lord in everything we do. By putting this verse at the beginning of our family constitution, we're showing the most important boundary line of all. We're saying to each other, "If you're not interested in serving the Lord, then you're out of bounds." And since it's in writing and we've all agreed to it, choosing to go outside the boundaries means you're choosing to walk away from the blessings we share as a family. That may seem harsh, and it may not work for your family, but after we talked it through, this made perfect sense for us, so that's how our family constitution starts.

There are four keys to a successful family constitution. The first key is to create a family mission statement. My friend Dan Miller, one of the leading career coaches in the nation, says that a good personal mission statement takes into account your skills and abilities, your personality traits, and your values, dreams, and passions. I think the same is true when you're writing a family mission statement. Your family has skills and abilities. Your family has a unique personality. Your family has values, dreams, and passions. Take the time to examine all these things that you share collectively and use that insight to figure out what purpose your family is here to accomplish. Then, write it down.

The second key to a good family constitution is to tailor this to your specific family. There's no single, one-size-fits-all constitution that works for every family, so don't try to rubber-stamp it. You can find all sorts of examples online to help steer you in the right direction, but this has to be custom-made for your own weird, quirky, unique family.

Third, and this may be the most important key, you have to live out your family constitution every day. If this document really does represent who you are as a family, then your lives need to reflect what it says. Your constitution can't say that your family is generous and mission-minded if you're not giving—not to mention tithing—and you haven't been on a mission trip in the last decade. You're writing down the reality, not some aspirational, fairy-tale vision of what you *wish* your family was like. This is crucial for parents, because the kids in the family are watching you. My daughter Rachel Cruze constantly reminds parents, "More is caught than taught." Your kids learn a lot more from what you're *doing* than what you're *saying*. If you want to teach them how to live according to your family constitution, then you need to live that way yourself.

This doesn't have to be a long, overly detailed list of rules and regulations, though. Our family constitution is simply a one-page document, but it's enough. Just as an example, I'll share a couple of things that we chose to spell out in our constitution. First, like we've talked about several times already, our family believes in good, honest work. The Bible says, "If anyone will not work, neither shall he eat" (2 Thessalonians 3:10). Our family takes that pretty seriously, so if one of the future grandkids ever decides that he wants to sit around and take it easy on the family's dime, he'll have a rude awakening. That kind of behavior will result in him no longer being able to participate in the family's wealth until he decides to get off his tail and get back to work! That's not because we're workaholics or slave drivers; it's because we believe in the value of work. We think God put each one of us on this earth to do something, and if all you want to do is sit around all day watching daytime television, you'll never accomplish your God-given mission. So, I'm not going to support that kind of behavior. And, no, I'm not talking about stay-at-home moms here. Moms in the home may have the hardest—and certainly most important—job of all! Sharon was a stay-at-home mom, and she worked incredibly hard to raise our three kids.

Also, as a family of evangelical believers, we believe that a man and woman who aren't married shouldn't live together. That sounds pretty old-fashioned these days in some circles. You can call me a dinosaur; I'm okay with that. It doesn't change the fact that our family values don't line up with that behavior, so the family wealth won't support that decision. It's the same with drugs. If Junior is on drugs, we can't pour our family's wealth into Junior's drug habit. That doesn't mean we won't do everything we can to help him, but giving an addict a big pile of money isn't really helping him, is it? Of course, we outline a path of restoration for the prodigal child too. We spell out how he or she can come back home to full participation in the family and the family's wealth. We love our kids, and we will always want them to come back home if or when they stray. We just can't financially support whatever bad behavior they may fall into. That's one way we actually show our love for them, even though it's hard.

The last key to a good family constitution is forming a family council to update and enforce the constitution with regular meetings. Your family should meet regularly to go through all of this and discuss anything that needs to be added, removed, or updated. As the kids get older or married, this circle may start to grow. Since mine is the first Ramsey generation to start this, the meetings are basically made up of me, my wife, my three kids, and their spouses. As my kids have kids of their own, this group will get bigger. That's normal, but it doesn't necessarily mean every family member several cousins deep has to show up. You just want to make sure that the whole family (at least the part governed by the constitution) has a voice and a vote.

THE LEGACY BOX: YOUR LAST, BEST GIFT

We have covered a lot of things in this chapter that you need to do as you work toward your legacy journey. As you pull all of these things together, you're going to end up with dozens of documents, records, account statements, estate-planning paperwork, advisor contact information, and a hundred other things. This stuff doesn't sound all that exciting, but your family's ability to quickly put their hands on any one of these things could be a major ordeal if or when something happens to you. As I wrote in *Dave Ramsey's Complete Guide to Money*:

> If you were to die today, would your spouse or other family members know where all your important papers, life insurance policies, bank account information, computer passwords, and final instructions are? In my years doing the radio show, I have talked to countless mourning spouses who have no idea how to put their hands on this information. On top of the crushing loss of their husband or wife, they are immediately thrown into a financial nightmare because they don't know what to do or how to access the accounts or where the final instructions are. It's a total disaster. After talking to those spouses, I decided I was absolutely not going to leave my wife in that position if something happens to me.[1]

That's when I decided to put together what I now call the Legacy Box.

Your Legacy, in a Box

The idea behind the Legacy Box is simple: Put all of your important paperwork and information in a single place so your spouse and loved ones can find it when they need it. This is important regardless of what Baby Step you're on. There is simply no better way to say "I love you" than to take this step to minimize the stress and panic your family will feel in an already exhausting situation.

Your Legacy Box should have dividers, folders, or envelopes for at least each of the following items:

- Executive Summary: a one-page document that gives an overview of the box's contents
- Legacy Letters: personal letters from you to each of your family members to be distributed upon your death
- Birth Certificates
- Social Security Cards
- Passports
- Marriage Certificate
- Auto Insurance
- Homeowner's/Renter's Insurance
- Health Insurance
- Long-Term Disability Insurance
- Long-Term Care Insurance
- ID Theft Protection
- Life Insurance
- Umbrella Liability Insurance

- Estate Plan
- Power of Attorneys
- Wills
- Funeral Instructions
- Financial Account Log
- Safe Deposit Log
- Monthly Budget
- Tax Returns
- Money Market Statements
- Mutual Fund Statements
- College Funds
- Retirement Accounts
- Rental Property Summary
- Car Titles
- Home Ownership Records
- Passwords/Combinations

If you take our class *The Legacy Journey*, we even give you a nice wooden Legacy Box, complete with divider tabs for each of these categories.

When you finally get everything together, you need to do a couple more things. First, make a copy of *everything*. Basically, you need to create a second Legacy Box with copies and put it in a different location. That way, if your house burns down, you'll have a backup of the entire set of papers. You can also make a digital copy by scanning everything and using digital folders for filing. Then you can easily put a copy of your digital Legacy Box in your safe deposit box on a flash drive or CD-ROM for safekeeping. I just don't recommend people keep their *only* copy of everything in the safe deposit box.

Emergencies happen every day at all hours; don't make your family wait until the bank opens to get to the information they need in an emergency.

Last, you need to make sure your family members know where to find your Legacy Box and how to use it. You might even want to do a dry run, just like a fire drill. I have one friend who likes to do this to his wife randomly. They'll just be sitting in the living room with their kids, and my buddy will say, "Okay, honey. I just dropped dead, and you need my life insurance policy. Go!" Then she jumps up and runs to the Legacy Box and pulls the form. Okay, that's kind of ridiculous, but, hey, at least she'll know exactly what to do and where to go if or when something ever happens.

The bottom line with everything in this chapter is that you will always be able to find reasons to procrastinate. Unless someone has a terminal illness, the thought of doing a will always seems to stay in the "important but not urgent" category. I want to encourage you to think of everything we discussed in this chapter as both important *and* urgent. Remember, none of us is going to make it out of here alive. We're all going to die one day. The only question is: What kind of legacy do you want to leave when you do?

As for me and my house, we will serve the Lord.

Called to Generosity

B ack in my college business and finance classes, I was
introduced to a fantastic, must-have, do-it-all, fictional
product called the widget. The widget is used in case studies
as an example of a generic product from a generic company.
If a company is doing really well, they're manufacturing and
selling a bunch of widgets. They're keeping their supply chains
fully stocked, and they're keeping a close eye on inventory to
make sure they never run out of widgets. I remember one
case study in particular that has really stuck with me over
the years:

There was this guy who started a business that grew bigger and faster than he could have imagined. He developed a
cutting-edge widget that was on its way to becoming a household name. Everyone loved his product—including him. He
liked to spend his free time wandering the aisles of his widget
warehouse, gawking at the thousands of cases of widgets that
lined the shelves. Every now and then, he'd pull a widget off

the shelf and open it up like he'd never seen one before. He felt like a kid on Christmas morning! This guy *really* loved his widgets.

As business picked up, he had to stuff more and more widgets into the warehouse, which was beginning to get cramped. He was just about out of room before he realized he needed to tear down the old warehouse and build a bigger, better, cutting-edge warehouse. He called in the best engineers from across the country and meticulously designed every square inch of the place. His new facility would store all the widgets he'd ever need! It was the world's first multistoried widget warehouse. Before long, other business executives were calling him and asking him how he'd managed to get so many widgets into one space.

Filling that giant warehouse took a while, but one day, the delivery guy came and put the last box on the last shelf. The place was completely full. The young businessman stood in the middle of the warehouse, beaming with pride and joy at how successful he'd become. For the first time in several years, he relaxed a little and began dreaming of all the fun things he could do. He was on top of the world! But then, just as he was heading to his car, God showed up and said, "You fool! This very night your life will be demanded from you. Then who will get what you have prepared for yourself?" (Luke 12:20 NIV).

Oh, wait a minute. Maybe that wasn't an example from business class after all. Maybe I heard it in Sunday school instead. It's The Parable of The Rich Fool from Luke's gospel, but it doesn't feel thousands of years old, does it? It shows the same kind of attitude we deal with today when it comes to wealth.

It's the story of a farmer whose ground produced an enormous amount of crops—what we'd consider to be wealth. The farmer grew so enamored with his surplus that he filled a barn. When that barn was full, he tore it down and built another one. Then, after all that effort, God took him home.

Now, there was nothing wrong with the farmer's crops, and there's nothing wrong with the wealth we build today. The problem comes when, like the farmer, we store up wealth because we worship it and the wealth is our only source of security. God calls this idol worship, not management or stewardship. We take our eyes off of God and off of those around us, and instead we focus on how rich we can get and how much stuff we can accumulate. That's a totally self-centered, self-absorbed attitude, and it's what I've been warning against throughout this book. Just look at what the farmer says in Luke 12:18–19: "I will do this: I will pull down my barns and build greater, and there I will store all my crops and my goods. And I will say to my soul, 'Soul, you have many goods laid up for many years; take your ease; eat, drink, and be merry.'" In the space of only two verses, the farmer says "I" or "my" eight times! From a legacy journey perspective, there's no stewardship, no US or THEM in this guy's mind. He's totally and completely wrapped up in himself and in his own twisted version of NOW and THEN. The problem is: It is so easy for us to fall into this same trap today. After decades studying God's Word on this, and after hundreds of conversations with godly millionaires and billionaires, I think I've figured out how to keep this attitude from creeping into our mind-set.

The answer is generosity. Generous giving is the antidote for selfishness.

PRINCIPLES FOR GENEROUS GIVING

Before we dive into some nuts and bolts of generous giving, let's take one last look at the legacy journey framework. First, there's what we call the **NOW** stage, which is taking care of our immediate family before we do anything else. That includes getting out of debt, getting on a budget, and clearing away any financial emergencies that may be keeping us from moving forward. Next is the **THEN** stage, which is when our heads come up and we're able to see down the road a bit. That's when we start investing for retirement, saving for the kids' college, and setting a vision for our future. That leads to the **US** stage, which is when we focus on our family. We start to look at our children, grandchildren, and even our great-grandchildren, and we realize that the decisions we're making today set the tone for our generational legacy. Then, once we know our family is taken care of and we've set a fantastic legacy in motion, we look around and start to see the whole world through God's eyes. We see needs we never saw before. We see ways we can help people next door and around the world. We see people who are starving, orphaned, sick, or hurting, and our response is, "I can help!" That's a great place to be. That's what we call the **THEM** stage because at this stage, you're not focused on yourself, your future, or your family; those things are already taken care of. At this stage, you're focused on how God can use you to impact the world.

We're Made to Be Givers

The key to having an enduring legacy is to practice generous giving throughout your life—at every stage of the **NOW–THEN–US–THEM** framework. Giving is a hallmark character quality of those who win with money. In fact, it's almost impossible to find someone you'd consider to be Christlike who is not a giver. That makes perfect sense, doesn't it? The Bible says that we are created in the image of God. The truth of our being—the innermost part of who we were created to be—is to be a reflection of God. Just breathe that in for a second. We get confused about our purpose all the time. So many times we ask someone *who they are*, and they answer by telling us *what they do*. We confuse our jobs with our purpose. I am a teacher, an author, and a radio host. More important than that, I'm a husband and father. But even more important than that, I am a follower of Christ, which means Christ is *in* me.

When you peel back all the layers, what you find at the very center of me should be the image of my heavenly Father. Scripture says, "For you created my inmost being; you knit me together in my mother's womb" (Psalm 139:13 NIV). I once heard Ray Bakke talk about that passage. He described this beautiful image of God sitting in heaven with knitting needles actually *knitting* your DNA double helix. That's such an amazing picture. God specifically, meticulously handcrafted every single one of us. And as He did, He infused us with His likeness. We are made in the image of God—and He is a giver. He gave the ultimate gift in His only Son. He gave us every single blessing we've ever had. We've said throughout this book that God is the Owner. That means everything we will ever have comes straight from His hand. Psalm 84:11 says, "The LORD will give grace and glory; no good thing will He withhold from those who walk uprightly." If He gives so freely and so richly, and if we're made in His likeness, then that must mean we're made to be givers too.

Giving Is an Expectation

I believe that giving is an expectation for God's people. If we truly want to be like Christ, then we need to follow His example in giving—and He gave *a lot*. Scripture consistently shows the connection between working, earning an income, building wealth, and generous giving. The apostle Paul told the church in Ephesus, "Let him who stole steal no longer, but rather let him labor, working with his hands what is good, that he may have something to give him who has need" (Ephesians 4:28). That one verse ties it all together pretty well. You work, you earn, you give. That's what the *Havdalah* service is all about, remember? We work to first fill our own cup, and then we keep pouring until there's an overflow to be shared with others. That overflow is for the good of other people.

But, like we saw in Chapter 4, we have to keep that cup in proper perspective. You and God set the size of your cup (the lifestyle and investing ratios), and what's left flows out to serve others (the extra giving ratio). Like I said before, you have to remember that this is a *cup*; it's not a thimble or a swimming pool. You should always size your lifestyle cup so that it is small enough to overflow, but not so small that your family will starve. I'll add one thing to that: It's also not a recirculating fountain. Once the overflow leaves the cup and spills into the bowl—meaning it's out of your hands—you can't take it back. You have to keep an emotional distance from what you've set aside for giving. That's why it is so important for you to spend plenty of time in prayer as you set your ratios. It keeps you from trying to reclaim the money you and God already decided to give away.

Giving Should Be Fun and Private

If we're properly managing God's resources, then we're going to be giving—and we're going to be excited about the opportunity. Scripture says, "God loves a cheerful giver" (2 Corinthians 9:7 NIV). The word *cheerful* comes from the Greek word *hilaros*, which is where we also get the word *hilarious*. When you read it that way, you could say that God loves a *hilarious* giver. Wouldn't it be cool if your church broke out in wild laughter and applause as the offering plate passed by? That's the spirit we're supposed to have when we get the opportunity to tithe and share our overflow.

The problem is, people get confused about why they should give. Some use their giving as a way to promote themselves or to help their reputations. Honestly, that makes me a little sick. That's no different than the Pharisees Jesus talked about who liked to say long, loud prayers on street corners just so people would see how "holy" they were (Matthew 6:5–6). So with rare exceptions, your giving should be done in private, and it should never be a spectacle. Jesus was perfectly clear about this:

> Be careful not to practice your righteousness in front of others to be seen by them. If you do, you will have no reward from your Father in heaven. So when you give to the needy, do not announce it with trumpets, as the hypocrites do in the synagogues and on the streets, to be honored by others. Truly I tell you, they have received their reward in full. But when you give to the needy, do not let your left hand know what your right hand is doing, so that your giving may be in secret. Then your

Father, who sees what is done in secret, will reward you. (Matthew 6:1–4 NIV)

Please don't get too caught up in the "reward" this passage mentions. That's not why we give. We give to help other people, not to help ourselves. This isn't a transactional thing where we're always trying to get a return on our giving. We should give because we're called to be givers, because we are passionate about using God's resources to serve other people. We've been blessed not only for our good, but also for the good of others. We are blessed *to be a blessing* (Genesis 12:2–3), and that's an exciting, win-win deal!

Charles Dickens said, "Do all the good you can, and make as little fuss about it as possible." Giving anonymously keeps our motives pure. It keeps us from making our giving all about me, me, me. And for those of us who are believers, that attitude leaves a wide-open door for people to experience God in a whole new way. When we lean into a big need, and we do it completely anonymously, who gets the credit? God does! If a struggling single mom finds a nice used car sitting in her driveway with the keys and title on the dashboard, she's going to tell the world that God provided big-time—if you're not standing in the spotlight. This all goes back to ownership and stewardship. The Owner, not the manager, should get the praise. If it's God's money (and it is), and if He is directing how you use it (which He should be), then He's the one who met that need—not you. Don't let your ego get in the way of a powerful testimony about how God showed up to change someone's life.

Giving Is about More than Money

I had a lady call my radio show recently with an interesting take on tithing. She said, "I've heard people say that you should give more than money, that your giving should also include your time and talents. Well, I work at my church, so I'm just going to count the time I spend there as my tithe."

I replied, "Well, you can do whatever you want, but that's not what the tithe is. Giving should include your time, your talents, *and* your treasure. So, biblically speaking, you should give your tithe—and why don't you give your time too? You're obviously good at drama; why don't you join the church's drama team?"

I was poking at her a little bit, but that call made me realize some people are confused about what giving is all about. Recently, my team and I have been discussing what biblical stewardship really means. We keep coming back to the idea that stewardship is handling all of God's blessings God's way for God's glory. And when we say "all of God's blessings," that's what we mean: *all* of His blessings. That includes more than our money. It includes the time He gives us on earth. It includes the skills, passions, interests, and opportunities He gives us. It includes *everything* we have to offer. Money is just one small part of that. That doesn't mean we can give our time and talents *instead of* our money. God's given it all; as good stewards, we should be giving some of *all* of those blessings.

Giving Unlocks Your Full Potential

You will never reach your potential level of creativity, talent, passion, success, or excellence until you learn to give. I know that's a bold statement, but I believe all of Scripture backs me up on this. Luke 6:38 says, "Give, and it will be given to you: good measure, pressed down, shaken together, and running over will be put into your bosom. For with the same measure that you use, it will be measured back to you." Please don't hear this as a cause-and-effect, give-to-get statement. I don't think that's what the passage means at all. Instead, I think it's talking about what happens in your spirit when you give. Read it again: "Give, and it will be given to you: good measure, pressed down, shaken together, *and running over* . . ." That kind of sounds like the overflow we've been talking about, doesn't it?

I think the inverse is true too. People who aren't givers, who are greedy and hold their money in clinched fists, never have an overflow. That's because they're not *flowing* at all; they're stopped up! When I teach budgeting, I always tell people that money is active; it is always moving from somewhere and to somewhere. From a legacy journey perspective, we might say that money should always be *flowing to us* and *flowing through us*. If we interrupt that flow by hoarding everything we get, then all we're doing is building bigger barns and stockpiling our wealth. That's a sick, twisted view of money. That's a picture of the manager trying to steal the Owner's resources, and that's not an attitude that God can bless.

Generous givers, however, are attractive. They have a spring in their step and an energy about them that draws people to them. They live their lives with open hands, and that changes one's whole perspective on life. Billy Graham once said, "God gives us two hands: one to receive with and one to give with." It takes both hands to create and leave a legacy, and you can't receive or give if your hands aren't open. An open hand is there to give money, sure, but it's also there for so much more. An open hand can lift someone out of a mess. An open hand can hug someone going through a difficult time. An open hand can applaud someone else's success without a trace of jealousy or envy. An open hand can serve the needs in the community. An open hand is ready to receive more and more of God's blessings because the person with an open hand can be trusted with more. Giving changes so much more than your money; it changes your life and sets you free to unbelievable levels.

WISDOM FOR RADICAL GIVING

I remember the first time someone explained the concept of the tithe to me. I thought it was a scam. I came to a relationship with Christ as an adult, so I was already working and doing pretty well at the time—before our bankruptcy. So here I am making a good income, enjoying all the fun things that money can buy, and suddenly I'm supposed to cut 10 percent of my income right off the top? And I'm supposed to give it to whom? To God? It didn't look like He needed my money. To the church? We were in a beautiful church with a multimillion-dollar building. It looked to me like they were doing better than I was. If God loved me and blessed me financially, why on earth would He make me give Him a huge slice of my money? I didn't get it . . . at first.

Giving for Dummies
I'll be honest: I don't have a full, detailed, expertly researched exegetical study on the tithe. I know people get into that sort

of thing, and I think it's great if that's your passion. For me, though, the tithe is pretty simple. Once I understood that God is a giver, and that I'm also supposed to be a giver because I'm made in His image, the reason for the tithe came into focus for me. I don't think God tells us to tithe because He needs our money or because His church would fall apart without it. I think He tells us to tithe because He wants to teach us how to flex our giving muscles. In my book *Dave Ramsey's Complete Guide to Money*, I explain it this way:

> I believe that God puts us through the mechanical act of giving—even when we don't fully understand the reasons why—because the act of giving changes us. It crushes our hearts and reforms us into something that looks and acts a little bit more like Christ. You can't say you're a follower of Christ when you're not giving. You can't walk around with the clenched fist and tell people about how amazing Jesus is. There's a disconnect. They won't believe you because your whole attitude is one of selfishness, fear, and greed. Remember, the clenched fist is the sign of anger. Jesus never talked to people about the love and grace of God with His hands balled up into fists!
>
> Every time I open my hand to put money in the offering plate at church, or to support a missionary, or to leave a huge tip for a struggling single mom waiting tables, it shifts how I see things. Every time I spend a weekend serving other people instead of skiing on the lake, it changes my heart a little bit. Over time, all those changes add up as we become more and more like Christ.

Because we are designed in God's image, we are happiest and most fulfilled when we are serving and giving.[1]

Giving is hands down the most fun I have with money. I get such a thrill when God uses me to help families or ministries do things they thought were out of reach. One of the highlights of my year is our company's annual Christmas party, which has become somewhat of a local legend. Our team works insanely hard all year. These are families at every point on the wealth spectrum. Some are working on their debt snowball with gazelle intensity, doing whatever is necessary to take care of their **NOW**. Others are doing really, really well in building wealth and are fully in the **THEM** stage of their legacy journey. A lot of them are somewhere in between. We might have the most random assortment of cars of any parking lot in Nashville, with twenty-year-old junkers parked next to high-end Mercedes up and down the rows!

Once a year, a couple of weeks before Christmas, every one of these families gets dressed up to attend the Christmas party. We rent out the nicest banquet room we can find, and a committee plans every detail, down to the minute. We treat these families to gourmet food and world-class entertainment, and we (literally) roll out the red carpet to make them feel like the superstars they are. Then, at the end of the night, it is my honor to stand on stage and give each of them their Christmas gift. We've done laptops, iPhones and iPads, televisions, game systems, vacations, cash—you name it. The single goal of the whole event is to make everyone feel loved and appreciated.

This one party is a huge line item on the company's budget. I won't tell you how much we spend on that event and the gifts, but I'll just say no one ever feels shortchanged. So, why do we do it? That party represents a ton of money that would otherwise go into my pocket and my leaders' pockets. Why don't we just give each team member a ham and keep the rest of the money? It's because almost thirty years ago God told me to start tithing. I wasn't a natural giver back then, but I was committed to following God's ways of handling money. That meant giving. When I started, it was just the tithe; that was the minimum, which is a good thing, because I don't think I could have afforded any more. But learning how to give, even only 10 percent, opened the doors to the most powerful, most exciting, most enjoyable part of building wealth: the opportunity to share it with others.

Giving above the Tithe

The tithe gets you started and helps you keep an emotional distance from your money. It teaches you how to give. That's why there's a 10-percent giving blank at the top of all of my budget forms. I don't care what Baby Step you're on, you need to be giving a tithe. It's not only important in your **NOW**, but it will gradually shape you into the kind of person you'll be later in your legacy journey. If you go through the process of building wealth with the purpose of leaving a legacy, your journey won't be **NOW–THEN–US–*ME***; it will be **NOW–THEN–US–*THEM***. That means giving well above the tithe—when you are ready.

But when are you ready? Extra giving above the tithe enters your plan after Baby Step 3, which means you're out of debt and you have three-to-six months' worth of expenses saved in an emergency fund. At that point, you haven't started building wealth yet, but you can start dipping your toes in the water of extra giving. Up until this point, you haven't had any overflow to share, but now your cup is about to start overflowing for the first time, so it's a great time to start sharing some of that overflow. You just can't go crazy with extra giving at this point, because you're still taking care of your family first. You have to make sure your **THEN** and **US** stages are taken care of not just for today, but for the future.

When you're pretty much finished with the **US** stage, here's what life looks like: Your retirement savings are maxed out. You and your spouse are going to be just fine heading into your retirement years. Your kids are going to have the money to go to college debt free. You have investments above your retirement accounts for the purpose of building wealth, which creates overflow. You're using budget ratios to keep everything balanced, including extra lifestyle, investing, and—that's right—extra giving. When you're at this point, it's time for your giving to come unglued. When you get to Baby Step 7, you have zero debt (including the house), and you're a wealth-building machine. That's when you get the joy and honor of practicing radical, extravagant generosity regularly. God may specifically call you to do some big giving before this point, and that's fine. Just consider those to be exceptions. But otherwise, save your mind-blowing level of giving for this stage, where your golden goose (your wealth) is laying enormous eggs that you can give and share freely!

Your Biggest Investment

"Dave, you're a *horrible* giver!"

That comment caught me off guard. You might think this

was said in the early days when I was still trying to figure out the tithe, but you'd be wrong. That comment came much, much later. In fact, it was just a few years ago. The problem wasn't that I wasn't giving; the problem was that I wasn't being a wise giver. Sharon and I were budgeting and living on budget ratios, but we weren't doing a good job directing all those giving dollars. In fact, too often that money would collect month after month, and I'd look up in December and get in a big rush to give it all away in time to get the tax write-off for the year. At that point, I'd just start writing checks to ministries without taking any time to get to know who they were, what they did, or how they handled their money.

I was talking about this with a friend who was further along in his wealth building than I was, and he said, "Dave, you're a horrible giver. You spend a lot of time on your business investigating every little thing. You spend a lot of time on your personal investments looking at charts and spreadsheets and lifetime performance. In those areas, you do due diligence because you're making an investment. But Dave, when you give, you're investing in the kingdom of God. That's the biggest investment you'll ever make! Why aren't you doing due diligence with that?"

As a math and business nerd, that question hit me like a ton of bricks. It was so obvious when he said it, but it's something I hadn't taken seriously before. From that day on, though, I started treating all my giving as investments. That meant I had to slow down, do my research, and pray. I had to really get in there and see what this money would do inside a ministry. If you are giving to a ministry that has bad operational and money-management practices, you may be harming them. You are in essence an enabler, just like if you gave money to a family who had poor spending habits. If your giving is a large percentage of the ministry's budget, are you artificially playing God in their planning? After facing these questions, we started to work really hard at investing God's money in ministries as if they were a business investment—because they are.

We ultimately created a family foundation to manage all of our giving. My oldest daughter, Denise, who had nonprofit experience, is the director of the Ramsey Family Foundation. Her full-time job is to explore every single organization our family donates to. Here's what I found out through this process: As a family, we had a good understanding of God's ownership, but we weren't being good stewards of His resources—at least in the area of giving—because we weren't doing a good job of managing His wealth for the good of others. Hiring Denise as the foundation director put that into perspective. We were paying her a salary to manage our giving budget. If she did a sloppy, lazy, haphazard job, then we'd probably fire her and find someone to do a better job. But here's the thing: That's exactly how God was viewing me! He's the Owner, and He gave me this wealth to manage, but I was doing a sloppy, lazy, haphazard job in this area! Making that connection flipped a switch in my brain, and since we started the foundation and began viewing these gifts as investments in the kingdom, we've been able to do more with those dollars than we'd done in all the years before. We were finally doing our giving like I teach people to do their budgets: on paper and on purpose—before we gave a dime.

Give to Your Passions and Values

There will always be causes, ministries, and charities that need your help. That is an enormous responsibility to us as we start to give outrageously. How do you decide which ones to help? How do you choose the right ones out of a million good choices? I've known a lot of wealthy people who get so worked up about this that they try to give to *everything*. They spread their giving a mile wide, which means they don't make a big impact in any one organization. That's not the strategy Sharon and I took when we started giving above the tithe. Instead, we decided early on that we wanted to go a mile *deep* with our giving dollars. We felt like God had given us the opportunity to make a huge difference in a small handful of ministries. Would you rather give $1 to a million charities or give $1 million to one? That's a personal question I can't answer for you; I can only tell you what we chose.

Learning to say no to a need we observe or a giving request is really hard for most people—including us. There are so many wonderful works going on around the world that are inspired and directed by God. So how can you possibly say no to them? We all realize we have a limited giving budget; the money is not infinite. We had to come to grips with the fact that, while we are managing God's money, we are not God. Once we got over our messiah complex, thinking we were God, we were released from the guilt of not giving to every valid, wonderful cause. Steven Curtis Chapman's song "God Is God (and I Am Not)" helps me remember this.

But we still had to figure out where to do our giving. As we prayed about it, we realized that God had given each of us specific passions and values. Sharon grew up in a small town with a fabulous local church, so she has a heart for supporting local church ministries. I came to Christ as an adult, so I'm big on evangelism. Those are big passions for us, so we let them guide our giving.

The same is true for your value system. Don't put money into something that goes against your values. For example, I don't believe people should go into debt. Big shock, right? That means I'm not going to give money to a ministry that is deeply in debt and about to go millions deeper into debt on a building campaign. That doesn't align with my value system. It is completely opposed to everything I believe about God's ways of handling money, so clearly, I'm not going to pour money into it. God gave me these passions and values for a reason, so I'm going to use them as a filter for my giving.

DISPLACERS IN A DIRTY WORLD

There are voices in our culture today who believe we should give everything we have away. We've talked about that more than once in this book. Maybe we've talked about it too much, but I know so many godly, generous men and women of faith who have been beaten up over this issue. They've heard it so often and from such well-respected people that this toxic message has crept into their own hearts. They look around at their success and start asking themselves if they're doing something wrong by having nice things. Even if they give away millions or even billions of dollars over the course of their lives, like my friend I told you about earlier, they still question whether or not they're being good stewards of God's resources.

Don't Give Away the Golden Goose

Let's go back to basics again. God is the Owner. I am the manager. He's given me a portion of His resources, and He's given me and my family the responsibility of managing it for Him in the way He directs me. If I bow to cultural pressure and give away all of my wealth, what am I really doing? I'm just surrendering my role as manager. I'm saying to God, "Thanks, but no thanks. I don't think I should be trusted with what You've entrusted to me, so I'm going to pass that responsibility on to someone else." But here's the problem: God didn't entrust that wealth to them; He entrusted it to me. It wasn't their responsibility; it was mine. He gave me a job to do, and I told Him no because I was scared or ashamed or guilty or whatever those toxic voices wanted me to be. It may not be a popular opinion these days, but I think that's dumb. That makes me a terrible steward, and if I care more about what other people think than I do about the job God's given me to do, maybe He really can't trust me to manage more.

It is practically impossible for your legacy to outlive you if you kill the golden goose. I talk about this in my book *More Than Enough*:

> If you want to be a powerful giver you should view your wealth as the goose and give the golden eggs. If you give away the goose, the golden eggs are gone and so is your ability to help others. Those of you who think "those nasty rich people should be made to give up the wealth they have earned" are not only stupid; your short-sightedness kills the goose, and the poor are not really helped.[2]

If you kill the goose, you get one good meal. If you keep the goose, you get egg after egg and meal after meal. What if you considered it your job to manage the goose and give away the eggs? Couldn't you do more?

Of course, there are times when God specifically calls certain people to give away everything. He's put that call on my friend Robert Morris, who I told you about before. But those calls are for specific people for a specific purpose at specific times. It's not the typical biblical model. If God puts that call on your life, and if that's your conclusion after spending days and weeks in prayer, then that's fine. I would never stand in the way of what God is calling anyone to do. I'm just saying that would be a very, very unusual calling, so I'd encourage you to talk to your pastor, friends, peer group, and maybe a few wealthy people of faith before taking that big step. And never do it just because you think it's a way to "trick" God into giving you more. He may, and He may not. If you give everything away, you need to be emotionally and mentally prepared to live in poverty the rest of your life—or at least to completely start over with nothing. You have no idea what God may have in store for you next.

The Displacement Method

I love Dallas Willard's perspective on this issue. In his book *The Spirit of the Disciplines*, Willard argues that if Christians view money as evil and filthy, then godly people should never have money. And if godly people never have money, we are effectively surrendering all the wealth of the world to the enemy. If the people of God pull out of the marketplace, we leave a hole in the world that other forces will rush in to fill. Somehow I don't think that's what God had in mind.

Instead, we should practice the displacement method. Here's what I mean by that: If you push a physical object into a crowded space, it pushes other things out of the way. It *displaces* whatever's in its way. My wife, Sharon, is a health nut. She runs, works out, does yoga, and eats a near-perfect diet. It drives me nuts. You'd think after all these years, I would have gotten healthier just by osmosis, but no such luck. She recently got a juicer, and that's when things got really weird. She's juicing *everything*! She's juicing things I'm sure God never intended to be juiced. I'm talking about broccoli and Brussels sprouts here. I love her, but some of this stuff is just gross. The worst part is, sometimes when she's done with her health shake, the glass it was in looks like it's covered in mold. It has green crud in the bottom and a thick, nasty film all over the inside of the glass. Just looking at it, you'd think you'd have to throw out the glass, but here's the thing: When she takes one of those grimy glasses and puts it in the sink with the water running and she leaves it there, at first, the green grime holds on tight while the clean water runs over it. After a minute, though, all that junk starts coming loose and flowing over the top and out of the glass. A few seconds later, you can't see any trace of her shake. Simply pouring clean water continuously into the glass displaces all the junk that was there a minute before. That's what we're called to do with the money God gives us to manage for His kingdom. We're supposed to go into a dark world with our time, talents, and treasure and engage the culture in such a way that we create displacement. And the more of that we do, the cleaner the society becomes. The more we surrender and pull back from that, the more the filth takes over—because one side is going to displace the other.

That's true spiritually too. You can put something good in and push something bad out. It works both ways. Good and bad things can knock each other out of the way. For example, I know a musician who is crazy about Jesus and loves making music. Even though he's a strong Christian, most of his songs are what most people would call "secular" hits, meaning they don't talk explicitly about his faith. However, this is a man of God serving with integrity in a business that's often filled with filth. When he has a hit song on the radio, even if he doesn't mention the name of Jesus, he is displacing other trashy songs that could have been taking up that airtime. The same thing happens when a Christian teacher steps into a classroom, or when a Christian businessman opens a business, or when a Christian politician runs for office. They don't have to put the name of Jesus on a campaign poster in order to make an impact for the kingdom of God. All they need to do is serve with excellence, keep their integrity, and maintain their commitment to God, and that alone makes a huge impact. Just by *being there*, they are displacing the forces of the enemy.

My goal is to equip an entire army of displacers—godly men and women who have been spiritually, emotionally, and financially set free—to be so radically generous that, together, we can move the needle in some huge area of need in the world. What if the church was known as the organization that ended the AIDS epidemic or that wiped out malaria? How cool would it be if God's people, using His resources His ways, changed the world like that? That's a powerful vision, and it's entirely possible—*if* we move past all the toxic messages the world is throwing at us right now.

EATING CAKE OR LIGHTING CANDLES

Starting today, there's a phrase I want you to watch out for in the media. It's something I hear at least weekly, and it always seems to get thrown out there whenever there's a story about a wealthy person giving away a lot of money. Are you ready? The phrase is "giving back." You've heard it before. A wealthy athlete makes a big donation to charity, and the talking heads on TV say something like, "He's been so successful. It's great to see him giving back!" They say it with a smile, but think about what they're saying. My friend Rabbi Daniel Lapin says "giving back" implies that someone *took* something. If I rob a bank and return some of the money, then yes, I'm giving some of the wealth *back*. But if I apply God's ways of handling money and therefore build wealth because I've proved to be a wise steward, then I can't *give back*. I can only *give*.

Enough for Everyone

Phrases like *giving back* in this context reveal a fundamental misunderstanding of the economy. Like I said, *giving back* implies that I took something. If I'm wealthy, then I got that wealth by *taking it out* of the economy. So, *giving back* must imply that I'm *putting wealth back into* the economy. That's just not how the system works. This is what some people call a "fixed pie" view of economics. That is, there is only so much wealth in the world, and the only way I can get wealthy is by taking money away from someone else. So, the wealthier I become, the poorer someone else becomes because there's only a fixed pie of wealth to go around. But that's a false view of economics. There's not a set amount of money in the world, and the reason the poor are poor is *not* because the rich are rich. There's more at work here.

Rabbi Lapin explains it as the difference between cake and candles. If we have a cake, there is a fixed, limited amount of cake for all of us to share. We might get a ruler and T-square to carefully measure each slice to make sure everyone gets a totally equal distribution. In that case, everyone would get exactly the same amount of cake, whether they were invited to the party or not. It doesn't matter if you're starving or stuffed, skinny or fat, diabetic or healthy—everyone gets the same size piece of cake. Period. That's what I think of when I hear people talk about "wealth equality," which we discussed earlier in this book.

That's one way of doing it. Here's another: When the cake comes out, it could be a free-for-all. Everyone can get as much as they want and leave little or nothing for the next person. Now I like cake, so I might cut off a huge hunk. If you're a few spots down the line from me, you're probably going to get a little less because I'll be in the corner licking frosting off my fingers. This is the view many in our culture today have of wealthy people. They see them as gorging themselves while everyone else at the party goes hungry. And honestly, that view makes sense if you think there's a set amount of cake—or wealth—to go around.

But Rabbi Lapin shows a problem with that way of thinking: There is no cake. Wealth is more like candles than cake. Have you ever been to a Christmas Eve service at your church? These are sometimes called candlelight services, because at some point, all the lights in the worship center are turned off except for one simple, small candle. I've been in some services where the room goes pitch black. I couldn't see two feet in front of my face. The only thing I could see was the one little flame all the way across the room. And then, that guy lights the candle of the person next to him. And that person lights another candle, and so on. Before long, you see candlelight moving down each aisle and up and down each row. By the time you get to the second verse of "Silent Night," the whole room is lit up by the soft, bright glow of hundreds of candles—and little kids are dripping hot wax on everything.

With that image in your mind, let me ask you a question: What happened to the first guy's candle? Did he lose anything by lighting another candle? The whole room is now burning bright because he shared his light, but he still has what he started with. He could light a million more candles, and it wouldn't hurt his light at all. The same is true with money. When I use money to serve you or when you use money to serve me, neither of us have lost anything. We can both get a lift. And if I take my candle outside and use it to start a bonfire, I'll have a great big flame—but that doesn't take anything away from anyone else. That's how money works. I can keep it, grow it, spend it, or give it all away, and it doesn't impact your money at all. But if we all work together, we can combine our efforts and light up the whole world. As believers who have been given the responsibility of managing God's resources, I think that's our calling.

CHAPTER NINE

A Legacy Worth Leaving

M y favorite hero from the Civil War era is someone you've never heard of. Clyde Eckles West was seventeen years old when he fought in the war. I won't tell you which side he fought for, because it doesn't matter. There were great men in blue, and there were great men in gray. And Clyde Eckles West was definitely a great man. By the time the war was over, Clyde had had enough of the fighting. A man of faith, he felt a strong call on his life to do something of great value for God's kingdom. As soon as he was released from the army, Clyde put everything he owned, including his precious leather-bound Bible, into two saddlebags and threw them on a mule. Leaving the war behind, he headed south—preaching all the way. For years, Clyde Eckles West took that mule from one town to another, proclaiming the name of Jesus as he worked his way through the South.

Over time, Clyde's preaching turned to teaching, and he started a couple of colleges—one of which is still open to this day. He finally settled down in Maryville, Tennessee. He got married. He had kids. And years later, with a legacy of preaching the name of Jesus, educating young minds, loving his wife, and raising some pretty incredible children, Clyde Eckles West passed away. Now, that story may not sound all that remarkable to you. I'm sure there were thousands of fine young men like Clyde back in those days, and any one of their stories could be as powerful or more powerful than the one I just told. There's one difference, though. There's something that always brings me back to this particular itinerate preacher. There's a reason the story of Clyde Eckles West is so important to me. You see, he was my great-great-grandfather.

If, like me, you have trouble backtracking through all the "great-greats," I'll just say that Clyde was my grandmother's grandfather. Several years ago, not long after my grandmother passed away, some of us kids and grandkids were at her home visiting. While we were there, someone suggested we take a few things to remember her by. Some of my cousins flipped through the photo albums, and others looked through her old jewelry for keepsakes. I'm not much for jewelry, but I am a book guy. I wandered into her home library and looked over the shelves. I've always thought that a person's bookshelves can tell you a lot about who they are and what they believe. Just about the only mementos I have from deceased friends and relatives are some of their old, beloved books.

As I looked over her books, I came across her old Bible. It was beautiful. I flipped through it and saw her handwritten notes and the passages she had underlined. They all pointed to a life well lived. I felt like I was holding on to the most important part of my grandmother. As I sat there with that precious book in my hand, I looked down and saw another leather-bound book that had sat on the shelf beside her Bible. I reached down and pulled it off the shelf, and my mouth fell open. I was holding the Bible of my great-great-grandfather, Clyde Eckles West. By that time in my life, I knew all about Clyde. I had heard the stories and had read his memoirs. I had actually read about this old Bible in his memoirs, how his church had given it to him and how much he treasured it. This was the Bible that he carried in his Civil War saddlebags as he rode from town to town preaching the Good News. I gently flipped through it, and I saw Clyde's handwritten notes and a couple of sermons held together by nineteenth-century paperclips. I felt like Indiana Jones when he found the Holy Grail! I just stood there speechless for a while, and when I left my grandmother's house that day, those two well-worn Bibles were under my arm. Clyde's Bible will always be one of my most treasured, precious possessions.

Flash forward a few years. My son and youngest child, Daniel, was in school at the University of Tennessee in Knoxville. Sharon and I were in town for the football game, and we had some time to kill. Maryville is pretty close to Knoxville, so Sharon suggested we drive over to visit my grandparents' gravesite. I knew where the cemetery was, but I had no idea where their graves were. I called my aunt once we got there, and she directed me to the right spot. While I stood there in front of my grandmother's grave, my aunt told me over the phone, "If you look up and to the right, you'll see some old, huge pine trees. A bunch of the family is buried up there too. You'll recognize some of the names."

By that point, I was curious, so I wandered up to those

pine trees and looked around. I spotted a few names I recognized, and then my eyes fell on one old tombstone that looked about 150 years old. I had a feeling in my gut about it, and sure enough, there lay the grave marker of Clyde Eckles West, my great-great-grandfather—the man who rode all over the South with a Bible in his saddlebags, a Bible that now sat in my bookcase. I just soaked it in for a while. This man took God's call seriously. This good man left an inheritance of faith to his children's children. Four generations later, his Bible is still preaching. Clyde never could have imagined that. He never could have known that a century and a half later, he'd have an heir who held his trusty old Bible and considered it a legacy. Clyde wasn't focused on that. He was just focused on leaving a legacy in the best way he knew how. He followed the Lord's directions, but he left the outcome up to God. He put his legacy in God's hands.

As I stood there looking at his headstone, thoughts kept running through my mind about the legacies we leave. Then I remembered the old story that motivational speakers used to tell about the numbers on a headstone. I've heard it all my life. They'd say something like, "When we die, we'll have two numbers on our headstone: the year we were born and the year we die. Those numbers are separated by a little dash. You don't get to decide either of those numbers, but you do get to decide what to do with the dash." The dash represents your life. Everything you have ever done or will do is represented by that little dash on your headstone. And all the great speakers ask the same question: "What are you going to do with your dash?"

As we bring *The Legacy Journey* to a close, I want to broaden the horizon a little bit. Your dash isn't your legacy. Your real legacy is what happens in your children's dashes and in your children's children's dashes. That's the inheritance Proverbs 13:22 talks about—the impact you have not just on your life, but also on the lives that come after you. The good news is that you get to choose today what your dash will be, and if you've made some mistakes, you get to correct them. Even if you think you've run your life into a brick wall, guess what? Your children have a clean slate. Your mistakes don't have to transfer to them. Your legacy might be setting your kids up to be the first generation to be debt-free, or to be free of several generations' worth of emotional baggage, or to be free of whatever you think has gotten in your own way. You can choose today to put an end to wrong views and wrong behaviors that might have derailed past generations in your family. You can choose to do things differently and safeguard future generations to do things even better. You can do "all things through Christ who strengthens [you]" (Philippians 4:13). You can choose today what kind of legacy you want to leave.

Make it a great one.

The Pinnacle Point

Chapter Excerpt from
Dave Ramsey's Complete Guide to Money

Special Note

The following is a full chapter excerpt from my previous book *Dave Ramsey's Complete Guide to Money*.[1] It provides a detailed explanation of the different kinds of investments I recommend for building wealth. I have inserted a couple of updates to the excerpt below to fill in some additional investing information. You'll see those additions in italics.

For more on the basic how-to issues around taking control of your money and building wealth, be sure to check out my books *The Total Money Makeover* and *Dave Ramsey's Complete Guide to Money*, as well as our classes *Financial Peace University* and *The Legacy Journey*. Find out more at daveramsey.com.

When I was a kid growing up in Tennessee, one of my favorite things to do was to go out with my buddies and ride bicycles. Now, my bike didn't have all the fancy gears and options that you see on bikes today. My bike had one gear.

And it didn't have a little engine to help it get moving. All it had was two little stumpy legs to get it moving. And those little legs had to work hard to keep that thing going, because in Tennessee, there aren't many flat stretches of land. You pretty much have two options: up or down.

I remember a million times as a kid, I'd be riding along and all of a sudden the road in front of me would just start going straight up. Sometimes it was too steep to pedal straight up, so I'd start steering right and left, swooping side to side to keep my momentum going. You've been there, right? I'd fight and fight to get up that hill and then . . . there it was. After all that struggling to get to the top of the hill, there was a moment where the hill leveled off for a second just before the downhill ride of my life began.

That's a great place to be, and I'm not just talking about bicycles here. I'm talking about that point in life where all the hard work and struggle is behind you, and all the fun is in front of you. That's the Pinnacle Point, and as fun as it was on my bike as a kid, it's even more fun in my financial life as an adult. In your money, the Pinnacle Point is the place when your savings and investments—after years and years of dedication and hard work—make more money for you in a year than you make for yourself. It's when your investments produce a higher return than your work. That's the best downhill ride you'll ever have.

THE TIME IS RIGHT NOW

This is one of my favorite topics, and it's one of my favorite lessons in our *Financial Peace University* class. But every time I start talking about investments or we get to this lesson in FPU, we always hear the same few objections, so let's just go ahead and get them out of the way.

"Oh, Dave, Investing Is So BORING!"

Every time I teach on investing, I can immediately spot the Nerds and the Free Spirits in the room. The Nerds perk up, pull out their pencils, and start to run the numbers in the margins of their notebooks. The Free Spirits? Well, they go to their happy places. I can see all the Free Spirits in the room start to float out of their bodies. Their eyes glaze over and, all of a sudden, they are running through a wheat field or singing in the rain in their minds. They just totally check out.

So here's my suggestion for those of you who find this stuff boring. When I use the word *investing*, picture a vacation home in the French countryside. Or picture a ski trip with your whole family in a beautiful chalet that you've rented for a month. Or picture your spouse being home with you to hang out, laugh together, and just enjoy life. That's what investing is all about. It's not about the dollars; it's about the kind of life you want to live later on. What you do today will determine that.

"I'm on Baby Step 1! I Can't Even Think about Investing Right Now!"

I know you may just be starting this whole process, and that's okay. Wherever you are in the Baby Steps, I'm on your team. But even if investing is a few years off, you need to learn some basics so you'll know what to do next as you knock out the Baby Steps.

I love to ski. In the snow, on the water, I don't care where.

201

I just like moving fast and having two long planks strapped to my feet. If you've ever been on skis, you know the first thing they tell you is that your whole body will go wherever you're looking. If you're looking straight ahead, you'll go straight ahead. If you look to the right, you'll drift right. If you look down, don't forget to tuck and roll, because you're about to hit the ground or water. That's true with your money too. I promise, if you do the things we teach, you're going to get out of debt and save up a full emergency fund faster than you ever thought possible. And when you do, it'll be time to invest for wealth building. So let's get your eyes on that goal, okay?

"Long-Term Investing Is Too Slow! I Want a Fast Return on My Money!"

The only people who get rich from get-rich-quick schemes are the people selling them. They play on your emotions, set you up for a quick return, take your money, and then leave you high and dry. And the truth is, risky investments have become a playground for people with gambling problems. Hoping to turn $100 into $1,000 overnight isn't investing; it's gambling. You've heard me say before that the stuff I teach isn't always easy and it isn't a quick fix, but it absolutely works every time.

KISS YOUR INVESTING

Back when I was just starting to sell houses, one of my biggest problems was that I talked too much. Hard to believe, right? More times than I'd like to remember, I just talked and talked and talked, and I ended up talking myself out of a sale.

The reason is that I was flooding buyers with information—more information than they wanted or even needed! I went on and on about all these features, contract issues, upgrades, neighborhood stats, and everything else I could think to say. Fortunately, I finally figured out how to shut up, but not before a lot of people missed out on some good houses just because I was overcomplicating the whole process.

Investing can be like that. Sometimes "financial people" come in and start talking about all the options, tricks, and strategies, and it makes our eyes glaze over. As a result, we either sign whatever they put in front of us, letting them make all our financial decisions, or we just decide it's not worth it and we walk away. Either way, we lose.

That's why I always recommend the KISS strategy for investing: "Keep It Simple, Stupid." No, this does not mean that you are stupid if you make simple investments! Just the opposite. I'm saying that people get in trouble when they overcomplicate things. I've met with a lot of really, really rich people over the years—multimillionaires and even several multi*billionaires*—and most of them have a simple, even *boring*, investment plan. They do the same few, simple things over and over again, over a long period of time. Why? Because it works.

But a lot of people truly believe that investing has to be complicated, or that there's some trick to it—as if there's one big secret to investing and those people who figure it out get to be rich. But nothing will send you to the poorhouse faster than stupid, long-shot, high-risk investments. It's like that old joke: What's the most common last words for a redneck? "Hey, y'all. Watch this!" In investing, I think the most famous last words would be, "Don't worry. I know what I'm doing!"

"Financial People"

Too often, we play these games because "financial people" sit across the table and talk down to us like we're children. That drives me crazy! A financial advisor is usually an invaluable part of your team, as long as he remembers what his primary job is: to teach you how to make your own decisions. You need someone with the heart of a teacher who will sit down with you and teach you this stuff so that you can then make your own decisions about how, where, and how much to invest. You should never buy any financial product or service if you can't explain to someone else how it works. That level of education is what you're paying your advisor for!

There are two words you should say to financial and insurance people who talk down to you or won't (or can't) teach you how their products work: *YOU'RE FIRED!* Remember, these people work for you. If they aren't doing the job you're paying them for, cut them loose. And if you need help, be sure to check out our list of Endorsed Local Providers (ELPs) in your area. We've handpicked excellent men and women all over the country to help you make your own investing decisions. You can learn more about that at daveramsey.com or, if you're in an FPU class, in the online resources for this lesson.

FANCY TERMS: $10 WORDS FOR $3 CONCEPTS

Whenever I write, one of my guiding principles is that I don't use $10 words or words that sound too highbrow or stuffy. There are a few investing terms, though, that might fall into that category, so I'm going to take a minute to lay them out for you.

Diversification: Spreading the Love

Diversification is one of those terms that financial people throw around just to sound impressive. Let me take the wind out of their sails by clearing this up. Diversification just means to spread around. It's a really simple idea. Basically, don't bet the family farm on a one-horse race. This is a financial principle you may have learned in Sunday school, even if you didn't realize it at the time. Ecclesiastes 11:2 says, "Give portions to seven, yes to eight, for you do not know what disaster may come upon the land" (NIV).

Grandma said it too, didn't she? She always said, "Don't put all your eggs in one basket." The problem is, if you put all your eggs in one basket, something bad might happen to the basket. If it does, then you lose all your eggs. In recent years, we've had a lot of bad things happen to a lot of baskets. We've seen 9/11, Katrina, political drama, massive unemployment, and even a full-blown recession slam into a lot of people's single baskets, breaking a lot of eggs. But those who spread out their investments over several different options were better protected. If you spread them out over a wide area, you won't lose the whole thing when something goes wrong in one part of it.

The bottom line is that diversification lowers risk. So basically, what we're saying is that investments are like manure. Left in one pile, it starts to stink. But when you spread it around, it grows things. I bet your financial guy never laid it out like that!

Risk-Return Ratio

With virtually all investments, as the risk goes up, so does the hopeful return. That is, if I don't take much of a risk, I'm not going to make as much money. All investing requires some degree of risk; there really is no sure thing. In my book *Financial Peace Revisited*, I explain it this way:

> The lion at the zoo is a pitiful sight—the king of beasts is eating processed food. You can see deep down in his soulful eyes that he misses the thrill of the hunt. Any of you who want a guarantee on your money need to understand that you are paying the same price as the lion.[2]

The only real method to totally guarantee you won't lose your money is to put it in a cookie jar, but your return will be equal to your risk: zero. Actually, the cookie jar can't even offer a foolproof guarantee if your house is robbed or burns down. Besides, earning zero return is the same as moving backward once you factor in inflation, which we'll cover in a minute.

When you lay out investment options, you start to see a progression of risk. You start with the cookie jar—no risk, no return. One step up from that is a savings account, which is fantastic for your emergency fund but a joke for your investing. Your money will be fairly safe, but you'll be lucky to make 2 percent on it. A step up from that would be a Certificate of Deposit (CD), which is not much better than a savings account. A few more steps leads you to a mutual fund. A little more risk gets into single stocks. A few steps later and you are into day trading, where, risk-wise, you completely jump off the cliff.

I don't recommend single stocks or day trading, or Vegas for that matter, because the risk is just too high. But I also don't recommend cookie jars or CDs for long-term (more than five years) investing. The sweet spot, which we'll talk about later, is mutual funds. That's a great balance of reasonable risk and excellent returns.

Inflation

Something that should be handled alongside risk-return ratio is inflation. This is something that is too often left out of risk calculations. When we talked about the cookie jar, we said that it was basically no risk, no return. But that's not really true. With inflation working against us, if we left $100 in a cookie jar for a year, we'd still have $100 a year later, but that $100 would be worth less.

Inflation has averaged around 4.2 percent over the last seventy years, according to the Consumer Price Index (CPI). So if your money is not earning at least a 4.2 percent return, you're actually losing money every year. In fact, once you factor in taxes on your growth, you really need your investments to make around 6 percent just to stay ahead of inflation. So if you stick with cookie jars, savings accounts, and CDs as your long-term investing strategy, your money will be relatively safe but inflation will tackle you from behind. You've got to see 6 percent as your break-even point, so a little risk is going to be vital to your long-term plan.

Liquidity

Liquidity is a funny word, but, again, the concept is simple. It just means availability. If you have a liquid investment, then you have quick and easy access to your money. The cookie jar is totally liquid because you can walk over and get your cash out whenever you want. A savings account is about the same, and a CD is fairly liquid even though there's a short time frame attached. Pretty much the least liquid investment is one that a lot of Americans own, which is real estate. If you're a homeowner, your house is likely your greatest investment, but it is not liquid at all. If an emergency came up, you'd have a tough time liquidating your house by tomorrow.

TYPES OF INVESTING

We can already see the ground rules for investing. We're going to keep it simple. We're going to find investments that show a good, reliable balance between risk and return. We're going to listen to advisors but make our own decisions. We're going to stay away from gimmicks and get-rich-quick schemes. We're going to keep our investments diversified. And, of course, we're going to stay ahead of inflation. Before we do any of that, though, we're going to make sure it's time for us to start investing. Investing is Baby Step 4, so before you start saving up for retirement, you are debt-free except for your house, and you have three to six months of expenses saved up in an emergency fund. If you've done that, then it's time to start investing. So let's look at some of the most common types of investing, or investing "vehicles."

CD: The Certificate of Depression

A CD is a certificate of deposit, typically at a bank. This is just a savings account. That's it. I always crack up when people tell me they have solid investment strategy, and then tell me all their money is in CDs. It's a *savings account*. The word *certificate* does not make it sophisticated; the certificate is basically a receipt showing that you made a deposit at a bank. Whoopee! My kids had savings accounts when they were six years old! That's barely a step up from a piggy bank!

A CD will give you a higher rate of return than a standard savings account because you'll be required to leave your money alone until the CD matures. You may get a five-year CD, which means you deposit the money for a guaranteed rate of return—and you can't take the money back out until it matures at the end of the five years. If you do, you pay all sorts of fees and penalties. Even without the fees, though, the CD gives you a lousy rate of return. At the end of the day, a CD requires you to tie up your money for a few years, but then it gives you practically nothing in exchange. I don't own a single CD I just don't see a need for them.

Money Markets

So what if you want to get *some* return on a pile of money you don't need *today*, but you know you'll need in a few years? This is like when you're saving up for a house or a car over three to five years. I use money market accounts for that. This is essentially a checking account that you open up with a mutual fund company. These are low-risk, and they offer about the same rates as you'd get with a six-month CD. However, your money isn't tied up and you have check-writing privileges (with no penalty) in case you need to access the account sooner than you thought. Just keep in mind that money market accounts are for *savings*; this is not an investment. That's why money markets with a mutual fund company make a great place to put your emergency fund. It keeps the money liquid while still giving you at least a little return.

Single Stocks

Single stock purchases give you a tiny piece of a company. The company issues a number of shares to sell to shareholders, and those shareholders jointly "own" the company. That's what it means when a company "goes public." They go from being privately held to being publicly owned through the issuance of publicly traded stock. The value of the shares is tied to the value of the company. If the company's value skyrockets, the value of each share—each individual piece of ownership—also goes up. That's good if you get in and out at the right time.

For example, let's say you were an Apple® fan in the early 1990s. The technology company was having some trouble back then, and the stock hit the low twenties per share around 1993. But for some reason, you had a good feeling about where the company was going, so you bought one thousand shares at $23 each.[3] By 2011, that $23,000 investment would have been worth somewhere around $350,000. Not bad, right?

But here's the reality: For every Apple, IBM®, or Google®, there are hundreds of publicly traded companies in bankruptcy, and it is impossible to know what the future holds for individual businesses. Remember Enron®? The collapse of that one company completely obliterated $74 billion of wealth in the four years leading up to Enron's eventual collapse.[4] More than twenty thousand former employees were thrown into years and years of legal battles and lawsuits just to get back a piece of the money they lost in company stock.

Why? Because they had put all their eggs in one basket, and that basket fell apart. The same could be true for any business, at any point in time. That's why diversification is so important, and single stocks are one of the most UN-diversified investments you can make. Stay away!

Bonds

A bond is a debt instrument by which a company owes you money. Instead of buying a piece of ownership, as with a stock, you're pretty much loaning a company (or the government, in the case of government bonds) some money. That means instead of becoming an owner, you become a creditor. Like I said in *Financial Peace Revisited*:

> When you purchase a bond, the company that issued it becomes your debtor. The income is usually fixed, but again, the value or price of the bond will go up or down according to the performance of the company and prevailing interest rates.[5]

I personally do not like bonds for several reasons. First, it's based on debt, and it's no secret what I think about debt—borrowing *or* lending. Second, bonds are high risk because the company's ability to repay your investment is tied to their performance. So in that sense, it's like a single stock and has no diversification. And last, the performance of bond-based portfolios is generally pretty weak. This is another one I just stay away from.

Mutual Funds: The Alphabet Soup of Investing

Now we come to one of my favorite vehicles for long-term investing, the mutual fund. I *love* mutual funds. They have excellent returns, and they have built-in diversification that keeps me from having all my eggs in one basket. The problem is, a lot of people are scared off because they don't understand what a mutual fund is. Heck, I graduated college with a finance degree and I still had trouble understanding it! It's really not that complicated, though, once you strip out all the highbrow financial lingo. Let's take a look.

Picture a big bowl in the center of a table. You and your ten best friends are sitting around the table. Everyone puts a dollar in the bowl. That bowl is a mutual fund. You and your friends have all contributed, so you have *mutually funded* the bowl. It is a *mutual* fund. Get it?

So, what's in the bowl? It contains little pieces of stock in a whole bunch of companies. Picture it like a bowl of alphabet soup. If you look in there, you might see an "I" floating around, which could be IBM. You could see a "W," which might be Walmart®. There's an "A" and an "M," so that could be Apple and Microsoft®. Just imagine several companies floating around together in the bowl you and your friends funded.

A professional portfolio manager manages the fund, making sure that only the best investments are in the bowl. And this guy isn't flying solo. He's got a huge team of Nerds working for him—the best, brightest, nerdiest Nerds in the world! If the fund includes tech stocks, he'll have a Tech Nerd. If it includes restaurants, he'll have a Restaurant Nerd. These specialists spend all day, every day, learning every detail about these companies and industries. They pass that information to the fund manager, and the manager uses it to keep the fund filled with the best of the best investments. That crack team of Nerds can do a lot better job than any average bubba sitting at home picking stocks using a dartboard and dumb luck!

What the fund does depends on the goal, or the *fund objective*. If our fund is a growth stock fund, the fund manager will buy growth stocks. If it's a bond fund, the manager will buy bonds. If it's an international stock fund, the manager will buy—can you guess?—international stocks. You're getting it!

Diversification is fantastic in mutual funds. Let's say I wanted to invest in some good ol' American companies. If I were using single stocks, I could put $20,000 in Ford®, for example. But what happens if Ford implodes? I lose all my money! We talked about that with single stocks. That's just too much risk. But instead of going all-in with Ford, I could get a mutual fund that has a little Ford in it, along with up to two hundred other great American companies. So if Ford's value goes way up, I still benefit because I have a little Ford in my mutual fund. But if Ford goes bankrupt, I won't feel that much of a loss because it's just one small part of my fund. The other two hundred companies in the fund can protect me from a loss because they're all in there together.

Now, is there some risk involved with mutual funds? Sure, there are no guarantees. But remember what we said about inflation? If you just park your money in a "safe" CD, you're already behind the curve because inflation will take your legs out from under you. Besides, if you are invested in mutual funds containing the best and brightest two hundred companies in the country and they *all* fail at the same time, you've got bigger problems than your mutual fund. That would mean the entire US economy has fallen apart, the stock market would be worth zero, and the FDIC would have collapsed—so your "safe" bank savings would be worthless too!

Mutual Fund Diversification

Like I said, there are different kinds of mutual funds, and they all have built-in diversification. But I still recommend you diversify a little further by spreading your investments out over four different kinds of mutual funds. I tell people to put 25 percent in each of these four types: growth, growth and income, aggressive growth, and international.

Growth stock mutual funds are sometimes called mid-cap or equity funds. *Mid-cap* refers to the fund's capitalization, or money. So, a mid-cap fund is a medium-sized company. These are companies that are still in the growth stage; that's why it's called a *growth* stock fund.

Growth and income mutual funds are the calmest funds of the bunch. These are sometimes called large-cap funds because they include large, well-established companies. These funds usually don't have wildly fluctuating values. That's good and bad; they won't shoot up as much when the market's up, but they also won't fall as much when the market's down. These are basically slow-moving, lumbering dinosaurs.

Aggressive growth mutual funds are the exciting wild child of mutual funds. They represent small companies (so they're often called small-cap funds), and these are active, emerging, exciting companies. This is the roller coaster of mutual funds. There will be really high highs, and probably some really low lows. I had one back in the 1990s that had a 105 percent rate of return one year, then lost it all the next year. You absolutely don't want to put all your money here, but you need some aggressive funds in your plan.

International mutual funds are sometimes called overseas funds, and they represent companies outside the United States.

I recommend putting a fourth of your investments in international funds for two reasons. First, you get to participate in the growth of some foreign products that you probably already enjoy. And second, it adds another layer of diversification just in case something weird and unexpected happens to the US stock market.

Picking Mutual Funds

Always look at the track record of mutual funds before you buy one. And make sure that it has a good track record over at least five years, preferably ten or more. My favorites are the ones that have been around more than twenty years and have proved themselves to be quality, reliable investments. I have some mutual funds that are more than fifty years old! Those may be harder to find, but they give you an excellent track record. Whatever you do, don't buy a fund that's less than five years old. These are babies! If you can't see a track record of at least five years, keep looking. If it's a fund that really interests you for some reason, just make a note of it and check it a few years later.

I personally like to find funds with a good track record averaging at least 12 percent. But every time I say that, I get a million emails from people saying, "BUT DAVE, you can't get 12 percent on your investments! Are you crazy?" No, I'm not crazy. I use 12 percent because that's the historical average annual return of the S&P 500®, which gauges the performance of the five hundred largest, most stable companies in the Stock Exchange. The average annual return from 1926, the year of the S&P's inception, through 2010 is 11.84 percent. Just keep in mind that's the eighty-year *average*.

Sure, within that time frame there are up years and some

down years. I'm not that interested in the performance of any individual years or even any short-term timespans, but just for fun, let's take a look at a few. From 1991–2010, the S&P's average was 10.66 percent. From 1986–2010, it was 11.28 percent. In 2009, the market's annual return was 26.46 percent. In 2010, it was 8 percent. See, this thing is up and down all the time, so 12 percent isn't really a magic number. But based on the history of the market, it's a reasonable expectation for your long-term investments.

Bottom line: Mutual funds make excellent long-term investments, but don't bother with them unless you can leave that money alone for *at least* five years. This is where you park your money for the long haul, looking toward retirement.

Update: Betas, Loads, and Low-Turnover Mutual Funds

Since we're getting our hands dirty with serious investing at this point in your legacy journey, let's look at some of the nerdier parts of mutual fund investing that I don't often dive into. We'll quickly cover the beta, load versus no-load, and low-turnover mutual funds.

The beta is the statistical measure of risk for a mutual fund. A beta of 1.0 mirrors the market. That means a fund with a 1.0 beta is exactly in line with the ups and downs of the stock market. Anything over a 1.0 is a little wilder and less predictable than the market average, and anything under a 1.0 is calmer than the market average. So, something like a growth and income fund, which is the slow-moving, more predictable fund, might have a beta of 0.8, meaning it's fairly safe. But an aggressive growth stock fund with a beta of 2.0 is really wild; it has twice as much risk as the market average. Those are fun and they can generate great returns, but you don't want your whole portfolio to be a roller-coaster ride. Remember the risk-return ratio and keep your funds balanced among the four types we've discussed.

Now let's deal with load versus no-load mutual funds. A load simply means a commission is charged when you purchase a fund. A loaded fund has a commission built in, and a no-load fund does not. That's the difference. Now, you may think it's better to avoid the commission, but that's not always true. All funds—both load and no-load—have maintenance fees and other expenses attached. Sometimes, you can buy a loaded fund—which is more expensive on the front end—that has really low fees. So, over the course of many years you end up saving money because you aren't getting hit as hard with fees every year. That's not always true, but it's been the case with several of my investments.

So which is better: load or no-load? There's no clear answer. The truth is, I own both. The trick is to dig into the details and explore each fund on its own without making a blanket assumption that no-load is the better deal. That's where a quality broker comes in. Just be sure to get someone with the heart of a teacher who can give you all the information you need to make your own decision.

The last type of fund I want to talk about is the low-turnover mutual fund. That's a fund that holds almost all the stock it pur-chases. It almost never sells the stocks inside the fund, which is why it's called "low turnover." Let me explain why this is helpful. Let's say you paid $200,000 for a rental house, and the value of that property increases to $300,000 over time. As long as you hold the property, you don't have any taxes on that increase. Taxes aren't due until you sell it and realize that gain, which results in capital gains tax. So in a sense, you have tax-deferred growth on that property, right?

The same is true if you buy a single stock that goes up in value. If *you buy a stock for $100 that goes up to $300 over twenty years, you don't pay any taxes on that gain until you sell. I don't recommend you buy single stocks, but remember that mutual funds are made up of a whole bunch of stocks. If it's a low-turnover fund, the stocks inside the fund are basically sitting there for a long time. They aren't being sold out of the fund, which means I'm not paying taxes on the gains as the stocks leave the mutual fund. So that's another way to help defer capital gains taxes on my investments. I love these kinds of funds and use them a lot.*

Rental Real Estate

Real estate can be a lot of fun, especially for old real estate guys like me. However, this is the least liquid investment you can make. You know what they call houses that sell fast? Cheap. Don't mess around with real estate until you are out of debt, have a full emergency fund, have maxed out your 401(k) and Roth IRA options, have paid off your own house, and have some wealth built up. Only *then* are you ready.

And, of course, don't even think about real estate as an investment until you can pay cash for the property. Never, never, *never* borrow money for an "investment." The risk is enormous. I've seen literally thousands of so-called investors lose their shirts in real estate because they bought houses when they were broke. If you start playing with rental real estate without any money, you will crash. I promise. That is *exactly* how I went broke and ended up in bankruptcy court myself. I know what I'm talking about here.

Update: Let me jump in with a few more details here. Since rental real estate is one of only two types of investments that I do (the other one is mutual funds), people often ask me for tips as they consider getting into real estate themselves. So, I came up with my Four Rules for Buying Rental Real Estate:

1. **Buy Slowly and Pay Cash.** *Like I already said, never use debt to finance an investment. That's a surefire way to lose your shirt in real estate. Move slowly, make wise decisions, and never get rushed into a surprise "deal of a lifetime." Do due diligence with every property, and always have a lot of cash on hand after the purchase. You'll need it for whatever rehab you plan to do to get the property ready to rent or sell.*

2. **You Make Your Money at the Buy.** *Don't talk to me about how this neighborhood is going to skyrocket in value, so you're going to overpay for a property today. If you're going to buy a piece of property, you need to make money on it the minute you close. You want to buy it so cheap that it's an instant win.*

3. **Pay No More than 70–80 Percent Market Value.** *This ensures you get a bargain and you make money the instant you buy it. Never even consider anything close to retail when buying investment properties. If I find something I like that we estimate to be worth $200,000 market value, I'll offer $140,000—and I'll pay in cash, and we can close this week. Do a lot of people say no? Yes, but I don't care. There are plenty of others who say yes.*

4. **Only Buy Properties in Your Area.** *Don't get into the long-distance landlord game. It's a nightmare. I own a lot of properties, and every one of them is an easy drive from my house. If you own it, you need to be able to drive by it whenever you want. Otherwise, you could have someone*

changing the oil of their Harley in the living room of a house you own five hundred miles away.

Annuities

I personally don't use annuities very much, but they are options and they do have a place in some people's investing strategy, so let's take a quick look. There are two types of annuities: fixed and variable. Fixed annuities are terrible. They're basically a savings account with an insurance company, and they pay somewhere around CD rates. They're really not that different from a CD you'd get from your local bank.

Variable annuities are the only ones I like. These are essentially mutual funds inside an annuity. The annuity provides some protection against taxes for the mutual funds inside, so if you've already maxed out your other tax-favored plans like a 401(k) and Roth IRA, then a variable annuity might make sense. There are fees involved, but in exchange for the fees, you don't have to worry about taxes on the investment. Plus, some variable annuities offer a guarantee on your principal. So if you put $100,000 in the investment and the value drops below that level, you'll still be able to get your $100,000 back out of it. They're not for everyone, but if you're further along in your investing, you may want to look into some quality variable annuities. Just don't buy an annuity with an investment that is *already* tax-protected. If the investment is already safe from taxes, the added fees of an annuity just don't make sense.

All That Glitters Is NOT Gold

I just might be the only talk radio host in the country that does not endorse gold! The reason is simple: Gold is a horrible investment! Here's the deal: Gold value has been rising since September 11, 2001. People started buying it more not because it's a good investment, but because of some false belief that if the economy totally collapses, gold will hold its value. If that were true, then gold coins would have become the dominant currency in New Orleans during the Katrina disaster! That's a great picture of a mini-economic breakdown. If you had been there at the time, I bet you would have gotten a lot more for a bottle of water than for a gold coin!

But let's look at the numbers. Gold was worth $21 an ounce in 1833, up to $275 per ounce by 2001, and then shot up to about $1,345 by 2010. Even including the crazy growth gold experienced in the first decade of this century, the 177-year track record for gold is just 2.38 percent. Would you look at a mutual fund with a 2 percent rate of return over the past 177 years? No way! Besides, if gold was *ever* a good investment, it doesn't make much sense to buy it at its 177-year high! You always want to buy low and sell high. Gold gives you the chance to do the opposite. That's a bad plan.

THE TORTOISE WINS

I have been blessed throughout my career to have had the chance to sit down and talk with a lot of wildly successful, super-wealthy men and women. I love those opportunities, and I always pull out a pen and some paper because I want to hear from them how they got where they are. I believe you'll stop growing the instant you stop learning, so I'm always looking for some new insight.

One day, I was talking to a really rich guy—I mean *billionaire* rich. We were having lunch, and I gave him my standard billionaire question: "What can I do today that will get me closer to where you are in your business and in your wealth building?"

He leaned back and said, "Okay, here are two things. First, I've never met anyone who wins at money who doesn't give generously. You've got to keep a giving spirit if you want to win long term." Hey, that's no problem. Giving is one of my favorite things in the world! Check.

"Second," he said, "I want you to read a book. This is my favorite book. I read it several times a year. I read it to my children, and now I read it to my grandchildren over and over. It will change your life, your money, and your business forever." Now I'm a huge reader, so I'm pretty excited at this point. This megabillionaire is about to tell me the book that changed his life. Let's go!

"Dave, have you ever read *The Tortoise and the Hare*?" Huh? A children's book? An old fable? What does this have to do with building wealth? I just sat there for a second trying to decide if he was kidding or not. He wasn't.

He leaned in and said, "Dave, we live in a world full of hares. Everyone's racing around doing all kinds of crazy stuff. They're running ahead and falling back, running ahead and falling back. They're going back and forth, side to side, and all in circles. But the tortoise just keeps moving forward, slow and steady. And you know what? Every time I read the book, the tortoise wins."

That phrase has been stuck in my head for years: "Every time I read the book, the tortoise wins." It's not about fancy options. It's not about jumping on every new and exciting investment that comes down the pike. True, reliable, long-term wealth building is surprisingly simple—and even a little boring. It's a matter of doing just a couple of things over and over and over again, over a long period of time. Eventually, over time, when it counts . . . the tortoise wins.

The Road to Awesome

Special Note

Like we discussed in Chapter 5, "Your Work Matters," how you spend your time at work over the course of your life plays a huge part in the legacy you leave behind. To help you learn how to grow in your passions and turn your career into a calling, here's a brief overview of the great book Start *by Jon Acuff.*

At some point, you might have stopped dreaming. If so, fear pressured you into a dull job with a steady paycheck, and before you knew it, you were stuck in average.

Get unstuck.

How? The best way to eat an elephant is one bite at a time, and the best way to move toward your life's calling is one steady step at a time. So focus on finding work that matters, and then shift into living out your dream with passion and purpose. This is called your Road to Awesome.

It won't be an easy trek, and you'll have to learn, edit, and master as you go, but pretty soon you'll be enjoying a successful harvest and guiding others along their own awesome roads. Changing the world starts with changing you. So get ready—your legacy awaits.

Age Doesn't Matter Anymore

We're going to talk about five stages that every successful life goes through, but before I lay those out for you, I want to give you a word of warning: It doesn't matter how old you are today. As recently as a generation or two ago, your age was incredibly important. People got out of school, took a job at a big company, worked there for forty years, and then retired. Back then, your career path followed your age almost in lockstep. In your twenties, you were a rookie still trying to figure things out. In your thirties, you were getting better and making choices about what you liked about your job and what you didn't. In your forties, you relaxed a little bit because you knew how things worked and you might have even gotten a promotion. In your fifties, all the hard work of the past couple of decades started paying off and you probably had the best income of your life. Then in your sixties, your career started winding down, you spent more time helping other people do their jobs, and ultimately you left the building with a pension and a gold watch. The end.

I've got good and bad news. The bad news is, those days are long gone. And the good news is, those days are long gone! The problem back then was that you had to figure things out in your twenties. If you didn't figure out your calling until you were fifty, the cards were stacked against you. It was hard to work your way into a job that late in the game. Not anymore! Nowadays, age is out the window and you can jump on the train at any point. Wherever you are in life, right now is the perfect time to start pursuing your passion and turn your career into a calling.

I can give you three reasons why age doesn't matter anymore. First, traditional retirement is dead. There's a whole generation of Baby Boomers who are realizing the finish lines they were promised simply don't exist anymore—and they never will again. People in their forties and fifties are getting laid off unexpectedly and having to start over again in the middle of their career. Others are a decade into one career and figuring out that they hate what they do all day. Twenty more years of that feels like a death sentence! So they're starting over too. The old finish lines are gone!

Second—and this is the really cool part—anyone can play now. The technological advancements of the past twenty years or so have done away with all the old gatekeepers that used to stand in the way of people chasing their dreams. If you want to write a book today, you don't need a publisher or professional marketing company. You can do it all yourself and promote it to millions of potential readers through social media. If you're interested in mobile app development, you can get all the training you need (mostly for free) online, build an app, and sell it directly to customers through Apple's and Google's app stores. Think about your favorite app or website. Chances are, you have no idea if the person who created it is sixteen or sixty. Even better, you don't care! You're just looking for a quality product, and you're more than happy to give your time, attention, and dollars to someone who can meet that need. That's a perfect environment for an entrepreneur with passion!

Third, hope is the new currency for people chasing their passions today. That sounds a little weird, so let me explain.

In the old system, someone may work forty years while nursing the dream to give their time and money to a good cause *someday*. They thought, *Once I retire, I'll be able to* . . . But here's the thing: We don't have to wait until *someday* anymore. The current generation doesn't want to change the world *eventually*; they want to change it *right now*. So they're leveraging their skills and talents along with today's resources to add their desire to serve into the work they're already doing. That's how you end up with a national shoe manufacturer who gives a free pair of shoes away for every pair they sell or a local coffee shop that gives a certain percentage of every sale to charity. It's amazing! But that's the kind of stuff you can do when you realize you're no longer part of an outdated system that says you have to go to school, then go to work, then retire, and then die. That's just not who we are anymore.

You Can't Skip Stages

The five stages are not based on age. You can follow this path at any time, no matter where you're starting from. But there is one catch: You can't skip the stages. It doesn't matter what you've done in the past; once you decide to start (or start over), you're going to walk through each of these five stages one at a time. Remember when Michael Jordan decided to be a baseball player? He was the best basketball player on earth; he was a master of that game. Did that mean he could jump right to the mastery stage of another sport? Uh . . . no. He spent some time with a minor-league team, performed horribly, and never got called up to the majors. The dues he had paid in basketball didn't transfer over to baseball. He couldn't skip ahead. Neither can you. The good news, though, is that these aren't decade-long stages anymore. You can't skip them, but you can shorten them.

NAVIGATING THE FIVE LANDS

So let's look at the five stages every awesome life goes through. Remember, age doesn't matter, but you can't skip the stages. You have to start where you are today. None of this is going to happen by accident either. Use these five stages as a map as you plan out the career side of your legacy journey.

Stage 1: The Land of Learning

Learning is where you begin again. Regardless of your age, your work experience, or the overwhelming odds against you, the Road to Awesome starts with rediscovering your God-given passions.

What do you love doing? Building decks? Caring for kids? Writing a blog? No book can spell out your life's passion. But that's okay, because it's already inside you. Just play around with the dreams you already have, and see what sticks. Experiment like crazy. Don't just try to *find* your purpose; *live* with purpose. Make your passions count whether you ever turn them into a career or not. God put those things inside you for a reason!

Finding your new beginning will also take time. Time, like purpose, doesn't just magically appear. It will take getting up early and going to bed late. It will take working harder than you've ever worked before. And it will take a ton of follow-through and a lot of frustrating firsts. So give yourself some grace. Too often, we think we need to have the finish line in place before we ever take the first step, but that's a trap. Stephen Covey says we should "begin with the end in *mind*," but sometimes we misinterpret that to mean "begin with the end in *stone*." You have no control over the finish line. The only line you can control is the starting line; that one is entirely up to you.

Start experimenting in this stage. Throw some stuff on the wall and see what sticks. Set some goals and start working toward them. But if you can't finish one thousand words per day on your sci-fi novel or attend five baking workshops a month, don't sweat it. This is just a time of exploration. Pat yourself on the back for what you got done and let the undone stuff slide. Pick it back up tomorrow, and most importantly—keep learning!

Stage 2: The Land of Editing

Editing is all about subtracting distractions. You're not adding new things to your dream here; you're removing things that are almost-but-not-quite the right things. This is where you start to separate the good from the great. This freaks a lot of people out, so let's make it simple. If you died today, what would you regret *not* doing? Spending more time with your family? Running a marathon? Opening your own coffee shop? These are your passions.

Next, ask yourself what might be the most frightening question of all: *Are these the things I'm doing now?* You see, we have a way of putting our dreams on a shelf and looking at them like museum exhibits, but we never actually do what it takes to make those dreams a reality. If you'd regret not spending more time with your kids, then here's an idea: Start spending more time with your kids *today*. You can't flip a switch and suddenly find yourself living in your passions, but you can (and should) start making the daily decisions that will ultimately lead you into your calling. That means you must make choices every day about whether to spend your time doing *this thing* that takes you further from your passion or *that thing* that brings you closer to your passion. That's what you do in the Land of Editing.

Stage 3: The Land of Mastering

You've found your passion. That's great, but don't quit your day job. First, you need to gain loads of experience—preferably without bleeding your bank accounts dry or cashing in your 401(k). It's hard to live with purpose if you can't pay your bills.

In his book *Outliers*, Malcolm Gladwell asserts that it takes ten thousand hours of hands-on experience to become a master of anything. That's a lot of hours, but it goes by fast. At a forty-hour-per-week pace, you'd hit the ten-thousand-hour mark in less than five years. Think about where you were five years ago. It probably doesn't seem that long ago. And the older you get, the faster it goes by. Why not spend that time gaining experience at what you're passionate about? You could be a full-fledged, world-class expert at it in just five years!

I'm not saying you should quit your day job tomorrow and spend the next three months sitting on your sofa dreaming. That's a mistake way too many people make. There are safer and easier ways to log some experience hours. Can you say "part-time job"? If your dream is to run a local coffee shop, maybe you should spend a few hours a week behind the counter at Starbucks just to make sure you like it. If you're going to hate it, let's hate it at that level, not after you've walked away from the safety net of a full-time job.

You could also volunteer somewhere that gets you closer to your passion, and you should spend time with amazing mentors. In all of this, your goal is to really get to know your dream and then get wildly, ridiculously good at it. This takes time. The fastest way to become an expert at your new calling is to do so slowly—by acquiring insane amounts of experience.

Stage 4: The Land of Harvesting

You're killing it. And you're making money! Sink your toes in the sand and sip from a coconut.

Not so fast. Farmers don't go on vacation during the harvest. Neither should you. This is the time to build upon your success and surround yourself with a circle of support to keep you grounded. Your spouse (or a close friend or family member if you're not married) is your inner circle of support. This person keeps your big head deflated and your bruised ego encouraged. Don't be afraid to lean on your rock.

Rely on your outer circle of support—friends and family—for celebrating milestones and learning from failures. And don't forget to support their dreams too. Fear fears community. So scare the tar out of it.

Stage 5: The Land of Guiding

Welcome to your legacy. It's time to guide.

You may not feel ready to guide others yet. That's okay; do it anyway. Guiding someone is as easy as starting a conversation and following through with your time. Mentoring doesn't have to be hard; it just has to be intentional. So mold the relationship to your comfort level, and tweak as you go. The goal here is to help someone else on their own road to awesome. You don't have to have all the answers, and you don't have to be the wise old man on the hill. Just be you—but be the version of you who's done what it takes to win and now has some wisdom to share. Remember how much it meant to you when someone a few steps ahead of you slowed down to walk with you for a while? Now it's your turn.

THE END OF THE ROAD?

Congratulations! Now you're officially awesome, and that's exactly what God wants for you. We shouldn't settle for "ordinary" because we don't serve an ordinary God. He didn't create you to be average; He created you to be awesome! But remember that the end is not really the end. It's easy to get stuck in your own success and accidentally stop growing in the process. Find something new to spark your interest, go back to the beginning if necessary, and keep on learning!

Notes

Chapter One

1. Reference to Joel 2:25: "So I will restore to you the years that the swarming locust has eaten."

Chapter Two

1. Albert Mohler, "The scandal of biblical illiteracy: it's our problem," Christianity.com accessed April 17, 2014, http://www.christianity.com/1270946/.
2. Ibid.
3. Morgan Housel, "Attention, protestors: you're probably part of the 1%," *Yahoo! News*, October 28, 2011, http://news.yahoo.com/attention-protestors-youre-probably-part-1-153806044.html.
4. Courtney Blair, "Compared to the rest of the world Americans are all the 1%," *Policy.Mic*, December 6, 2011, http://policymic.com/articles/2636/compared-to-the-rest-of-the-world-american-are-all-the-1.

Chapter Four

1. Daniel Lapin, *Thou Shall Prosper* (Hoboken, NJ: John Wiley & Sons, 2002) 150.
2. Robert Morris, *The Blessed Life* (Ventura, CA: Regal Books, 2002) 179.

Chapter Five

1. Earl Nightingale, *The Strangest Secret*, Keys Publishing, Inc., 1956, compact disc.
2. Robin S. Sharma, *The Monk Who Sold His Ferrari: A Fable about Fulfilling Your Dreams and Reaching Your Destiny* (Fort, Mumbai: Jaico Publishing House, 2003).

Chapter Seven

1. Dave Ramsey, *Dave Ramsey's Complete Guide to Money* (Brentwood, TN: Lampo Press, 2011) 168–169.

Chapter Eight

1. Dave Ramsey, *Dave Ramsey's Complete Guide to Money* (Brentwood, TN: Lampo Press, 2011) 312.
2. Dave Ramsey, *More than Enough* (New York: Penguin Books, 1999) 269–270.

The Pinnacle Point

1. Dave Ramsey, *Dave Ramsey's Complete Guide to Money* (Brentwood, TN: Lampo Press, 2011) 195–216.
2. Dave Ramsey, *Financial Peace Revisited* (New York: Viking Penguin, 2003) 146.

3. Kathy Rebello, Peter Burrows, and Ira Sager, "The fall of an American icon," *Business Week*, February 5, 1996, http://www.businessweek.com/1996/06/b34611.htm.

4. Kris Axtman, "How Enron awards do, or don't, trickle down," *The Christian Science Monitor*, June 20, 2005, http://www.csmonitor.com/2005/0620/p02s01-usju.html.

5. Dave Ramsey, *Financial Peace Revisited* (New York: Viking Penguin, 2003) 129.

TAKE THE NEXT STEP
Join *The Legacy Journey class today!*

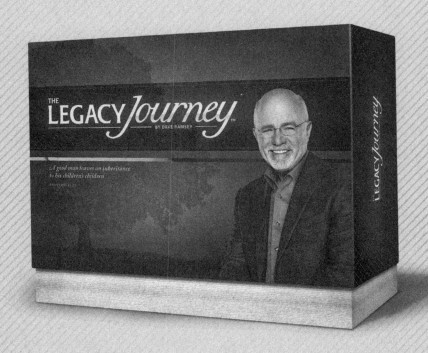

Taught by Dave Ramsey, America's trusted voice on money and business, *The Legacy Journey* is a seven-week, biblically based class that will teach you how to change your family tree and leave a legacy for generations to come. It will lead you deeper into investing, basic estate planning, purposeful living, and safeguarding your legacy. You'll also discover the keys to building generational wealth, protecting your relationships, and living a life of true generosity.

The Legacy Journey provides a biblical framework for how to live now so that you can leave a personal and family legacy and impact the kingdom of God like never before.

Start your journey today at daveramsey.com/legacy